Canadian Celebrity Readers

Famous Female Athletes

Grades 4-8

Written by Ruth Solski
Illustrated by Dan Day

About the author:
Ruth Solski was an educator for 30 years. She has written many educational resources over the years and is the founder of S&S Learning Materials.
As a writer, her main goal is to provide teachers with a useful tool they can implement in their classrooms to bring the joy of learning to children.

ISBN: 978-1-55495-007-2
Copyright 2009
All Rights Reserved * Printed in Canada

Published in Canada by:
S&S Learning Materials
15 Dairy Avenue
Napanee, Ontario
K7R 1M4
www.sslearning.com

At A Glance

Learning Expectations	Scott, Burka, Magnussen, Manley	Cindy Klassen	Sandra Schmirler	Myriam Bédard	Karen Cockburn	Elaine Tanner	Chantal Petitclerc	Silken Lauman	Perdita Felicien	Nancy Greene	Beckie Scott	Abigail (Abby) Hoffman	Hayley Wickenheiser	Marnie McBean and Kathleen Heddle	Catriona Le May Doan	Beverly Boys and Sylvie Bernier	Vickie Keith	Carolyn Waldo and Michelle Cameron	Bobbie Rosenfeld	Beth Underhil
Reading Comprehension																				
• Recalling specific details	•				•	•		•	•	•			•				•		•	•
• Locating proof		•																•		
• Classifying information			•											•	•	•				
• Evaluating information				•		•					•						•			•
• Using context clues							•													
• Expressing an opinion								•	•		•							•	•	
• Recalling specific details											•							•		
• Sequencing details in order															•					
Vocabulary Development																				
• Identifying word meanings	•			•	•						•							•	•	•
• Identifying parts of speech	•	•				•				•										
• Identifying base words	•		•	•							•						•		•	
• Antonyms, synonyms, homonyms, homophones		•	•		•				•	•		•	•		•		•	•		•
• Creating a paragraph			•																	
• Syllabication, compound words					•	•	•											•		
• Prefixes, Suffixes						•														
• Alphabetical order						•														
• Blends, Digraphs, Vowels											•	•			•	•			•	
• Developing writing skills															•		•			
Research Skills																				
• Using the Internet to locate specific information		•		•	•				•				•				•			

Canadian Celebrity Readers
Famous Female Athletes

Table of Contents

About this Book:

This book is a compilation of twenty biographies and twenty worksheets pertaining to famous Canadian female athletes. The biographies have been created to promote Canadian female athletes who perform and compete in a wide range of winter and summer sports and to provide an interesting genre to strengthen students' reading skills. The worksheets that accompany the biographies focus on the development of a variety of reading comprehension skills, the development and reinforcement of vocabulary and language skills, and the continuing development of research skills.

Ways to Use the Biographies and Worksheets

1. **Reproducible Worksheets:** Reproduce each biography and worksheet and staple them together to form a handout. The students read the biography, discuss the information and then complete the activities on the worksheet.

2. **Laminated Folders:** Each biography and its worksheet could be reproduced and glued to the inside of a file folder. A photograph of the female athlete obtained from a sports magazine or the newspaper or from the Internet could be glued to the front of the file folder. Multiple folders on each athlete may have to be made depending on the size of the group or the class.

Example:

The file folders should be laminated to ensure longer usage. The folders could be placed at an Interest Centre in the classroom. Each student chooses a folder on one of the athletes, reads the biography, and records the answers to the worksheet in a notebook or workbook

3. **Discussion Topics:**

- list different types of sports
- classify them as summer or winter
- list training equipment necessary
- disadvantages of being an athlete

- types of competitions
- training requirements for each sport
- advantages of being an athlete
- characteristics of a good athlete

One of Canada's most famous and sensational figure skating champions of the 20th century was Barbara Ann Scott. Her wonderful performances, girlish beauty, and sparkling personality captured the hearts of fans around the world. At the age of 11, Scott defeated skaters twice her age to become the youngest junior champion in Canadian history. When she was 15, Scott claimed the Senior Ladies Championship and the next year won the North American Championships.

In 1947, at the age of 18, Scott won the European Championships and was the first Canadian to do so. Several weeks later, she won the world championships, which brought greater international recognition to Canadian skaters. In 1948, Scott had her most glorious year. She reclaimed her world title and at the Olympic Games, she was first in school figures and gave a dazzling performance on an ice surface that had many imperfections, winning Canada's first Olympic gold medal in figure skating.

During the sixties, a figure skating dynamo by the name of Petra Burka was making a statement on the ice. In 1962, when she was 15 years old, Petra became Canada's Junior Ladies Champion and placed fourth at the World's Championship in Prague. From 1964 to 1966, Petra was Canada's reigning Senior Ladies Champion. At the 1964 Olympic Games in Innsbruck, Petra skated a dazzling performance and won the bronze medal. In 1965, she became a triple crown champion winning the Canadian, North American and World Figure Skating Championships. During The World Championship in Colorado, Petra was the first woman to complete a triple Salchow jump in competition.

Canada's next figure skating inspiration was a bright and vivacious girl from Vancouver by the name of Karen Magnussen. She became Junior Champion in 1965 and was Canada's reigning Senior Champion from 1968 to 1973. During the year of 1971, Karen won the championship crown for the last North American Championships. At the Olympic Games in Japan in 1972, she captured the hearts of Canadians when she won the silver medal of these games. In 1973, Karen skated a spectacular performance at the World Championships in Bratislavia, Czechoslovakia and became the third Canadian woman to be crowned World Figure Skating Champion.

During the 1980's, a petite, bubbly blonde by the name of Liz Manley from Ottawa exhibited grace, speed, and incredible jumping ability on the ice. In 1979, while still a junior, Liz was the first Canadian woman to land a triple jump combination, a triple Salchow followed by a double loop. In 1981, Liz won the bronze medal in the senior division and for the following years of 1985, 1987 and 1988, she was Canadian Champion.

The highlight of Liz's skating career came in 1988 at the Calgary Olympics. Liz had experienced some difficult times during her skating career and no one expected her to be a contender for a medal. She was sitting in third place after her school figures and short program. Her electrifying performance in her long program, which included five triple jumps, captured her a silver medal and made her a national celebrity. ✪

Scott, Burka, Magnussen, Manley

Name: _____ Date: _____

Reading Skills

Name that Skater! On the line provided record the name of the figure skater that answers each question.

Which female skater:

1. was known for her incredible jumping ability?

   _____

2. was the last woman to win the 1971 North American Championships?

   _____

3. was the youngest Junior Ladies Champion ever in Canadian history?

   _____

4. was the first woman to complete a triple Salchow jump during a competition?

   _____

5. won Canada's first Olympic gold medal in figure skating?

   _____

6. won an unexpected medal at the Calgary Winter Olympics?

   _____

7. was the third Canadian woman to become a world champion?

   _____

8. opened the international door for Canadian skaters?

   _____

9. was the first Canadian woman to land a triple jump combination?

   _____

10. was a triple crown champion?

   _____

Vocabulary Skills

A. Match each word in the box to its meaning. Record the word on the line provided.

celebrity	contender	spectacular
dynamo	dazzling	vivacious
imperfections	sensational	

1. causing excitement _____

2. to inspire admiration _____

3. having flaws or defects _____

4. having surplus energy _____

5. full of life; lively _____

6. exciting qualities _____

7. competitor; challenger _____

8. a famous person _____

B. Underline the nouns and circle the adjectives in each sentence.

1. Her wonderful performances, girlish beauty, and sparking personality captured the hearts of fans around the world.

2. Karen Magnussen was a bright and vivacious girl from Vancouver.

C. Record the base word for each of the following words on the lines provided.

1. contender _____

2. national _____

3. sensational _____

4. wonderful _____

5. girlish _____

6. dazzling _____

7. imperfections _____

*C*indy Klassen is a Canadian speed skater and Canada's most decorated Olympian. At the age of two, Cindy was introduced to hockey by her father. When she was five, she began playing hockey and soccer with local clubs. During high school, Cindy was an avid athlete who tried to squeeze in as many sports as she could. Although she had a wide variety of interests, her main focus was hockey.

Cindy played boys' hockey during most of her life and reached the double and triple A levels in her home province of Alberta. She thrived on the intense training that she received from the hockey coaches. Her goal was to play on the women's hockey team for Canada at the Olympics in 1998. During 1995, Cindy played on Manitoba's female hockey team and when she reached the age of 16, she switched to Senior Women's hockey and was chosen to play on the Junior National Team at Lake Placid in the United States in 1996. Things were moving along as she hoped until 1997, when she was not selected for the 1998 Olympic Women's Hockey Team.

With her Olympic dream destroyed Cindy was devastated and depressed. What was she to do now as she did not have an alternate plan? Her parents encouraged her to take up speed skating since her skating skills were so strong. Her immediate reaction was not a positive one. When Cindy was younger, she and some of her hockey friends had made fun of the long blades and skin tight outfits of speed skaters. After giving her parents' suggestion some thought, Cindy decided to give speed skating a try. Off she went to the Susan Auch Oval thinking speed skating would be a breeze. Much to her surprise, Cindy found it was harder to do than it looked but with the encouragement of the various coaches, Cindy rapidly improved.

In a year, Cindy was on the roster for the Manitoba long-track team that was to compete at the Canada Winter Games in 1999, in Cornerbrook, Newfoundland. Unfortunately, the ice melted and the long-track events never took place. Cindy did compete at various Canada Cup events and earned a spot on the Junior National Team in February of 1999. At this competition, she won the 1000 meter race and took third place in the 500 meter race.

In the year 2000, Cindy made the National Team and in 2001, she earned three top 10 finishes at the World Single Distance Championships, including a bronze in the 1500 meter race. In 2002, Cindy collected a bronze medal in the 3000 meter race as well as fourth place finishes in the 1500 meter and the 5000 meter races.

Cindy was flying high and on her way until one day during training, she experienced a dreadful mishap. While rounding a corner, Cindy crashed into a group of skaters. Her right arm was cut from her wrist to the elbow by a skater's blade. It sliced through 12 tendons, a nerve, and a major artery. Everyone felt that Cindy's skating season was over but two months later, she was training again with a splint on her arm. Cindy's 2004 to 2005 season was very successful. She won the World Cup title in the 1500 meter as well as first place in the 1500 meter and 3000 meter at the World Single Distance Championships.

At the 2006 Winter Olympics in Torino, Italy, Cindy won a bronze medal in the 3000 meter, a silver in the 1000 meter as well as a team silver in the Pursuit. She struck gold in the 1500 meter race which was her specialty. In her most dreaded race the 5000 meter she won a bronze.

Cindy Klassen will go down in the Canadian sporting records as the first Canadian Olympian to win five medals in one Olympic Games and the only Canadian with six Olympic medals. ✪

Cindy Klassen

Name: _____   Date: _____

Reading Skills

Locate a sentence in the biography that proves each of the following statements about Cindy Klassen are true. Record the first six words of the sentence on the line provided.

1. Cindy Klassen had a goal in mind while she played boys' hockey.

   _____

2. Cindy found out that long range plans don't always come true.

   _____

3. Cindy's parents were supportive and tried to help her?

   _____

4. Cindy's negative response to her parents' suggestion was for a reason.

   _____

5. Speed skating is a difficult sport.

   _____

6. Cindy's strong skating skills and her eagerness to work helped her speed skating to move quickly.

   _____

7. An unfortunate accident almost ended Cindy's speed skating career.

   _____

8. Cindy Klassen is a determined and feisty athlete.

   _____

9. Cindy Klassen is Canada's most decorated Olympic athlete.

   _____

Vocabulary Skills

A. Use the following pairs of antonyms to complete each sentence.

most - least	happy - depressed
strong - weak	easy - difficult
positive - negative	

1. Cindy's reaction to her parents' suggestion went from _____ to _____.

2. Although speedskating looked _____ to do, Cindy found it _____ at first.

3. Cindy was _____ with her hockey career's direction but became _____ when she didn't make the Olympic Women's Team.

4. Cindy's skating skills were _____ but her speedskating style was _____ at first.

5. She won gold in her _____ favourite race and bronze in her _____ favourite race.

B. Underline the words that best describe Cindy Klassen's personality.

energetic	lazy	loses interest
avid athlete	courageous	fearless
weak	able to focus	positive
insecure	disinterested	fickle
goal oriented	successful	hardworking
thinker	fighter	

Research Skills

Using the Internet or the resource centre, research to find out the answers to the following questions.

1. What is speedskating?

2. What are the different types of speedskating?

Sandra Schmirler and her curling rink (team) won the hearts of many Canadians and raised the profile of women's curling at the national and international levels. She was the skip of the most dominant rink in women's curling worldwide during the 1990s.

Sandra Marie Schmirler was born on June 11, 1963 in Bigger Saskatchewan and was the youngest of three daughters. As a little girl, Sandra was actively involved in many sports, but loved playing hockey the most. At the age of 12, Sandra began curling in Grade 7 as part of the school's physical education program. During high school, she played as third on her school's curling rink and won a provincial championship in Grade 12. After graduating from high school, Sandra went on to study Physical Education at the University of Saskatchewan. She curled with a team who made their first appearance in Saskatchewan's provincial playdowns in 1983.

Sandra moved to Regina after graduating to take a job at the North West Leisure Centre. She continued to curl and was nicknamed "Schmirler the curler" by a fellow employee at the centre. In 1987, as a member of Kathy Falman's rink, Sandra won her first provincial championship. On this team, she met Jan Betker who became a close friend and life-long curling partner.

In 1990, Kathy Falman's team had a disappointing performance at the provincial championships and Sandra decided to form her own team. She recruited Jan Betker as third, Marcia Geidereit as lead, and Joan McCusker as second. These four women made an awesome curling team. They won three Canadian Championships known as the Scott Tournament of Hearts in 1993, 1994, and 1997, and the World Curling Championships in the same years. This was a feat that no other women's team had ever done. No other women's team made up of the same four members had ever won more than one world title. Sandra also became known as

the Queen of Hearts due to her rink's repeated victories at the Scott Tournament of Hearts.

In 1997, as well as winning Worlds, the Schmirler rink won at the Canadian Olympic Curling Trials, which earned them the right to represent Canada in curling at the first medal events at the Nagano Games in Japan. The Schmirler rink was well respected in Canada and the world curling circles due to their great curling skills, but also for their humble, down-to-earth attitudes, and warm personalities. At the Nagano Olympics, the Schmirler rink won gold and was vaulted into international fame and Sandra became known as the Queen of Curling.

After all the media frenzy, accolades from the Premier and the Mayor, and celebrations were over, Sandra returned to a normal life with her husband and daughter. During her second pregnancy, Sandra suffered from an agonizing pain in her back which did not go away when her second daughter was born. She was diagnosed with a type of cancer which she fought courageously, but lost the battle at the age of 36 on March 2, 2000.

Tributes to Sandra appeared in newspapers across the country from sports writers and public figures. Buildings, parks and streets now bear her name in Regina and Bigger, Saskatchewan. A fund, called the Sandra Schmirler Foundation, was established by the Scott Paper Company to help babies in crisis at neonatal centres in hospitals across the country. Every time a Canadian thinks of curling, watches it, or plays the game, Sandra Schmirler will be remembered. ✪

Sandra Schmirler

Name: _____   Date: _____

Reading Skills

Classify each statement pertaining to Sandra Schmirler as true or false. Record the correct answer on the line provided.

1   Sandra Schmirler took over Kathy Falman's rink because it was having a bad season.
_____

2.   During Grade 12, Sandra developed a passion for curling.
_____

3.   Sandra's rink was made up of Jan Betker, Kathy Falman, Joan McCusker, and Marcia Geidereit.
_____

4.   For three consecutive years, Schmirler's rink won the Canadian Curling Championships.
_____

5.   The four women on Schmirler's team were humble, honest, and down-to-earth players.
_____

6.   Schmirler's rink was highly respected by fellow curlers and fans around the world.
_____

7.   Sandra and her team mates were the first Canadians to compete for medals at the Olympic Games in curling.
_____

8.   Schmirler's team won the silver medal for curling at the Nagano Olympic Games.
_____

9.   The world of curling was deeply saddened when the death of Sandra Schmirler was announced.
_____

10.   Unfortunately, all of Sandra Schmirler's contributions to the world of curling have never been recognized.
_____

Vocabulary Skills

A. Complete the following paragraph about the game of curling with the words located in the box.

second	skip	brooms	granite
house	target	turns	sweepers
team	two	players	rectangular

Curling is a _____ sport played by _____ teams, each having four _____ on a _____ sheet of carefully prepared ice. The teams take _____ sliding heavy, polished _____ stones down the ice towards a _____ called the _____. Two _____ with _____ follow each stone directing it to its resting place. Each team consists of a lead, a _____, a third, and a _____.

B. Classify each pair of words as S for synonyms, A for antonyms, and H for homonyms.

1. raised, lowered _____
2. competition, tournament _____
3. pain, pane _____
4. most, least _____
5. partner, associate _____
6. feat, feet _____
7. due, dew _____
8. feat, accomplishment _____
9. remembered, forgotten _____
10. friend, buddy _____

A biathlon competition consists of a race in which contestants ski around a cross-country track where the distance is broken up by either two or four shooting rounds, half in a prone position and the other half standing at designated targets. The contestant with the shortest total time wins.

For many years, only men competed in the biathlon at the Olympics. It was not until the 1990s when women began to compete and Myriam Bédard was one of them.

Myriam Bédard was born on December 22, 1969 in Neufchâtel, Quebec and was one of four children of Pierre and Francine Bédard. Myriam was a very athletic child who played basketball, did gymnastics, and trained as a figure skater. When she was 14 years old, Myriam joined the Canadian Army cadets with some friends, where she learned how to shoot a rifle. During her cadet training, Bédard participated in a mixed relay team race at the cadet winter games. She was on a team with three men and played with borrowed equipment. Although her cross-country skiing skills were weak, her shooting skills were excellent, her team won the race and Myriam found a new sport.

In order to become a biathlete, Myriam had to improve her cross-country skiing skills. She also found out that being a biathlete is physically demanding and mentally challenging. As a biathlete, Myriam discovered she must study each course carefully and plan every part of the race ahead of time. Winning a biathlon is unpredictable, as the weather and the athlete's mental and physical condition on the day of the race can affect the outcome.

In a short time, Myriam began to do well at women's biathlon competitions. In 1987, she won a first and a second at the first Canadian Junior Biathlon Competition. During 1988, Myriam won the Canadian Junior title, two North American Championship races and a first and a second in Canada Cup tests. At the Junior World Championships in 1989, she finished fourth in the sprints and also won a Canadian senior title that year.

Being of very small stature and only weighing 115 pounds, Myriam trained hard to improve her upper body and her skiing skills, but finding money for her equipment and coaching was still a very big issue. Finally, her agent negotiated a deal with Metropolitan Life, Myriam's employer, which funded her training and equipment and a job when she retired from the sport. This deal allowed Myriam the freedom to buy her own custom rifle and enabled her to train with qualified coaches.

During the 1993 season, at the World Biathlon Championships, she won the gold medal in the 7.5km race and silver in the 15km race. Bédard was the first North American to accomplish this goal. During the same season, she placed second in the World Cup standings.

Myriam continued to work hard to increase her aerobic skills and physical strength in order to get ready for the 1994 Olympic Games in Lillehammer, Norway. During the 1994 Olympics, Bédard's training paid off and she achieved the goals that she had set for herself. She won gold medals in both the 15 km race and in the 7.5 km event. At the World Cup during the same year, Bédard won a silver medal in the 15 km event.

For her superior accomplishments, Bédard was named Canadian Female Athlete of the Year and awarded the Lou Marsh Trophy, which is Canada's premier athletic award. She also received the Velma Springstead Trophy for best Candian Female Athlete and was the first biathlete to become an honoured member of Canada's Sports Hall of Fame. ✪

Myriam Bédard

Name: _____   Date: _____

Complete the following activities with sentence answers.

1. Describe a biathlon competition.
   _____
   _____
   _____

2. Why is being a biathlete a difficult sport?
   _____
   _____
   _____

3. How does a biathlete have to prepare for a race in a competition?
   _____
   _____
   _____

4. What other factors may affect the outcome for a biathlete on the day of the competition?
   _____
   _____
   _____

5. What did Myriam Bédard have to do to improve her abilities as a biathlete?
   _____
   _____

6. What was the major problem affecting Myriam's progress in the sport?
   _____
   _____

7. How did Myriam get the necessary support for her training?
   _____
   _____

8. What results did Myriam Bédard's hard work achieve in 1994?
   _____
   _____

Vocabulary Skills

A. Using a straight line, match each meaning to the correct word.

1. result; outcome   prone
2. tallness   premier
3. lying face down   negotiate
4. excellent; very good   issue
5. first in rank of importance   unpredictable
6. to run at full speed   superior
7. uncertain; changeable   sprints
8. to talk over   stature

B. Skim through the biography to locate words that are antonyms to the following words. Record the antonym on the line provided.

1. decrease _____
2. inferior _____
3. junior _____
4. slavery _____
5. longest _____
6. upper _____

C. On the line provided, record the base word for each of the following words.

1. competition _____
2. contestant _____
3. athletic _____
4. equipment _____
5. physically _____
6. unpredictable _____

Research Skills

Using the Internet or the resource centre, research the biathlon to find out in which country the competition began and why it became a popular sport.

Karen Cockburn is a Canadian trampoline gymnast. She is a legend in the trampoline event and has been the best trampoline gymnast in Canada for 12 years. Since she has been on the national team, she has overcome many obstacles during her rise to the top of the trampoline world and has achieved national and international recognition. Her efforts have made her a great ambassador for Canada and the sport of trampoline.

Karen was born in Toronto on October 2, 1980 and was raised in the suburb called North York. Her athletic career began with the sport of diving. She used the trampoline during her training to simulate a diving board. At the age of 11, Karen switched from diving to artistic gymnastics. It was then that she realized the competitive trampoline was her true calling.

Karen was selected to join the Canadian National team when she was 14. One day, during training in 1995, Karen accidentally stepped on a ball while practising on the trampoline. She seriously injured her knee and had to have reconstructive surgery. Her injury kept her from training and competing for a year. She returned to the competitive trampoline world wearing a knee brace until 1999.

Karen developed a reputation throughout the trampoline world as being able to land her flips exactly where she planned on the trampoline. She also is known for her strong competitive drive that provides her with the energy to perform some of the most difficult routines in the world.

Karen has dominated the trampoline gymnastics sport in Canada, winning the national title nine times. In the 2000 Olympic Games held in Sydney, Karen came home with a bronze medal. Four years later in the Athens Olympic Games, she performed a difficult trampoline routine that secured her a birth in the finals. She won a silver medal and was the first trampoline gymnast to win two Olympic medals.

In 2003, Cockburn won her first world title. Since then, she has won dozens of World Cup medals. Karen is also part of a world class women's synchronized trampoline team. Her partner is Rosannagh MacLennan and together they have won eight World Cups in a row and captured gold at the 2007 World Championships. At the 2008 Summer Olympics in Beijing, Karen qualified for the finals in 4th place and won a silver medal in the women's final. She is the only trampoline athlete to have won a medal at every Olympic Games. Karen was chosen to carry Canada's flag during the closing ceremonies of the Beijing Olympics.

Karen's accomplishments have brought many aspiring trampolinists to the various clubs in Canada and have helped with the recognition and awareness of the sport of trampolining.

On December 22, 2007 Karen married her fellow-Olympian and former training partner Mathieu Turgeon. Karen's biography, entitled Karen Cockburn: Flying High, was published in November of 2007. ✪

Karen Cockburn

Name: _____   Date: _____

Reading Skills

Answer each question with a complete sentence.

1. What special skill made Karen Cockburn a famous trampolinist?

   _____

   _____

2. Why is Karen Cockburn able to perform such difficult routines?

   _____

   _____

3. What previous sport introduced Karen to the trampoline?

   _____

   _____

4. How has Karen been an ambassador for the sport of trampolining?

   _____

   _____

5. In what other sport is Karen also involved?

   _____

   _____

6. How successful have Karen and Rosannagh been as a team?

   _____

   _____

7. How successful has Karen Cockburn been as a trampolinist?

   _____

   _____

8. What honour was Karen Cockburn given at the Beijing Olympics?

   _____

   _____

Vocabulary Skills

A. On the line provided, record the number of syllables that you hear in each word.

1. trampoline _____   6. recognition _____

2. international _____   7. ceremonies _____

3. synchronized _____   8. obstacles _____

4. reconstructive _____   9. competitive _____

5. ambassador _____   10. simulate _____

B. Skim through the biography and find a word that matches each of the following meanings.

1. an old story _____

2. used for tumbling _____

3. a type of operation _____

4. to act like _____

5. happened at the same time _____

6. someone's life story _____

7. rebuild _____

8. badly _____

Research Skills

Using the Internet or the resource centre, research to find out the answers to the following questions. Use these key words: trampoline, trampolining

1. Who invented the trampoline?

   _____

2. Where did the inventor get this idea?

   _____

3. What are the various moves and positions used by gymnasts on the trampoline?

   _____

   _____

   _____

Elaine Tanner was one of Canada's greatest and most versatile swimmers in history. She made one of the biggest impacts in the water of any Canadian swimmer ever. Elaine specialized in the backstroke, the butterfly, and the individual medley. She earned the title "Mighty Mouse" due to her small stature of five feet and her competitive drive.

Elaine began swimming at the age of six and was a natural in the water. In no time, she was winning medals at various competitions. When her family moved back to Vancouver, she joined the Dolphin Swim Club and was coached by Howard Firby, who recognized her talent and inspired her to strive for greatness.

In 1966, at the age of 15, Elaine leapt to national attention when she competed at the Commonwealth Games in Jamaica, winning four gold medals, three silver medals, and seting two world records. Elaine and her teammates won the freestyle race and set a world record. She was honoured to stand with the relay team on the winner's podium and watch Canadian history take place as Canada's new maple leaf flag was raised for the first time at an International Games.

During the 1967 Pan Am Games in Winnipeg, "Mighty Mouse" put on a fantastic performance in the 200 meter backstroke. The spectators cheered, shouted, and stamped their feet in excitement when Elaine was in the lead and then when the electronic time showed that she had beat the world record, their cheers almost lifted the roof off the building. At these games, Elaine also won a gold medal in the 200 meter backstroke and two silver medals for the 100 and 200 meter butterfly.

At 17, Elaine was Canada's best hope for a gold medal at the 1968 Olympics. Her coach was not allowed to be involved in her training and his replacement was not experienced nor qualified. In 1968, the Olympics were held in Mexico City. The pressure on Elaine to win gold was enormous. An entire nation expected her to win. Elaine competed well winning all her heats and semi-finals and set two Olympic records. On the day of her 100 metre backstroke event, the team coach told her to change her style. Instead of using her usual fast start, he advised her to start slower due to the high altitude. Elaine was nervous, stressed, and also very obedient and she did what she was told. As a result, she lost the race everyone expected her to win. To this day, she does not remember receiving the silver medal or standing on the podium as she was in shock and traumatized by the media's hurtful questions and remarks when she got out of the pool. Even though Elaine arrived home with three of the five medals Canada had won, she felt she had let her country and its people down.

Elaine retired from competition at the age of 18. The devastation from losing the gold and the media's comments and remarks left deep scars on Elaine Tanner's spirit. Since then, she has suffered from depression, anorexia, had two failed marriages, worked at a series of jobs, alienated herself from her family and children, and even lived in her car for awhile. In 1987, she met a man by the name of John Watts whom she credits with saving her life.

Elaine Tanner's career may have been brief but in this short time, she won 17 national titles, 6 commonwealth medals, 5 Pan Am medals and 3 Olympic medals. She was the first woman to win four golds at the Commonwealth Games. In 1966, Elaine was the youngest person to be named Canada's best female athlete. In 1970, she was made an Officer to the Order of Canada and in 1971, she was inducted into the Canadian Sports Hall of Fame. ✪

Name: _____   Date: _____

Reading Skills

Answer each question with a complete sentence.

1. How do you know Elaine Tanner was one of Canada's greatest swimmers?
   _____
   _____

2. Does size make any difference to the performance or the results of an athlete?
   _____
   _____

3. Why did Elaine Tanner achieve such success in the pool?
   _____
   _____

4. What special historical event took place at the Commonwealth Games for Elaine and her teammates?
   _____
   _____

5. How did spectators react when Elaine Tanner competed successfully?
   _____
   _____

6. Why did Elaine lose the gold medal at the Olympics in Mexico in 1968?
   _____
   _____

7. Do you think if Elaine had followed her heart and swimming style, she would have won the gold medal?
   _____
   _____

8. Why do you think Elaine Tanner had a difficult life after the Olympics?
   _____
   _____

9. How can media comments affect an athlete?
   _____
   _____

Vocabulary Skills

A. Locate compound words in the biography to match each meaning. Record the word on the line provided.

1. to swim on one's back _____
2. athletes on a team _____
3. an unrestricted manner _____
4. the name of an insect and swimming stroke _____
5. a group of British countries _____

B. Locate the following common nouns in the biography.

1. the symbol of a country _____
2. an athletic award _____
3. a competitive group _____
4. large container of water _____
5. athletes stand on it _____

C. Locate the following proper nouns in the biography.

1. the name of a country _____
2. an island country _____
3. a Canadian city _____
4. an Olympic city _____
5. winter and summer games _____

D. Locate the words in the biography that are synonyms for the following words.

1. largest _____
2. tallness _____
3. real _____
4. ability _____
5. great shock _____
6. permitted _____
7. huge _____
8. uneasy _____

*C*hantal Petitclerc is a Canadian wheelchair racer and has had a very successful career in this sport. She was born on December 15, 1969 in Saint-Marc-des-Carrières in Quebec. At the age of 13, while playing with some friends on a farm near her home town, a heavy barn door fell on her. She was paralyzed from the waist down and lost the use of her legs. During an interview, Chantal stated that she always accepted her accident but the first year of her recovery was the hardest. While attending high school, her physical education teacher convinced her to take up swimming to develop her physical strength and stamina. This was Chantal's introduction to sports and to training.

While attending Laval University in Quebec City, she was introduced to wheelchair sports by trainer Pierre Pomerleau. Chantal took part in her first race, using a homemade wheelchair and came dead last trailing way behind the other competitors. It was then that Chantal fell in love with this sport and thus began the dazzling climb of this Canadian athlete as a specialist in wheelchair racing.

At 18, Chantal participated in her first formal wheelchair race in Sherbrooke, Quebec and returned with the title "Most Promising" and a real racing wheelchair. Chantal competed in many Canadian competitions, proving that she had the talent and the determination to reach the podium.

While developing her skills as a wheelchair athlete, Chantal pursued her studies in social science at the Sainte-Foy College and then studied history at the University of Alberta where she was able to train with Peter Eriksson, a former world class speedskater, who became her coach.

In 1992, Chantal participated in the Paralympic Games for the first time in Barcelona, Spain. She returned with two bronze medals that began her collection of 21 Paralympic medals. Chantal has also participated in competitions of all distances such as sprints, middle-distance races, and marathons. In the T4 class, Chantal holds the Canadian record in all the events and the record in the world 100 meter race. At the Atlanta Paralympic Games in the United States in 1996, Chantal won gold medals in the 100 and 200 meter events

and three silver medals in the 400, 800, and 1400 meter races. As well as individual races, Chantal has won wheelchair marathons in many cities across Canada.

At the Sydney Paralympics in Australia, Chantal won two gold and two silver medals in wheelchair racing. Her most remarkable exploit was at the Olympic and Paralympic Games in Athens, Greece in 2004, when she won five Paralympic gold medals and a first place in the 800 meter race in the Olympics, which was a demonstration sport.

The Summer Paralympics in Beijing, China, in 2008, was to be Chantal's last competitive games. Her glorious career came to a close with five gold medals. Chantal Petitclerc's determination, perseverance, and success has made her a super role model for all Canadians, those with and those without disablilities. Hopefully, Chantal's dream of the day, the International Olympic Committee granting wheelchair racing official Olympic status, will come true in the near future. ✪

Chantal Petitclerc

Name: _____   Date: _____

Reading Skills

Complete each sentence with the correct words from the biography.

1. Chantal Petitclerc was _____ at the age of 13 when a heavy _____ _____ fell on her.

2. Chantal took up _____ to improve her _____ and _____.

3. During one of her earlier races, Chantal used a _____ _____.

4. Chantal raced in _____, middle-distance races and _____.

5. In her first Paralympics in _____, Spain, Chantal won _____ _____ medals.

6. At the Atlantic _____ Games in the _____ in 1996, Chantal won two _____ medals and three _____ medals.

7. At the _____ Paralympics, Chantal won _____ gold medals and two _____ medals in wheelchair racing.

8. During the Paralympics Games in _____, Greece and _____, China, Chantal came home with ten _____ medals.

9. While training to become a wheelchair _____, Chantal studied _____ science and _____ at university.

10. Chantal Petitclerc is a fantastic _____ _____ for all Canadians.

Vocabulary Skills

A. In each of the following words, circle the prefix, underline the root word, or box the suffix.

1. remarkable   5. swimming

2. hardest   6. recovery

3. trailing   7. specialist

4. international   8. successful

B. Divide each of the following words into syllables on the line provided.

1. paralyzed _____

2. interview _____

3. competitor _____

4. determination _____

5. individual _____

6. marathons _____

C. Record each group of words in the correct alphabetical order on the line provided.

1. wheelchair, won, waist, world, where

   _____

2. friends, farm, former, future, first

   _____

3. status, stamina, sports, strength, specialist

   _____

4. middle, many, marathons, meter, medals

   _____

5. competed, coach, competitors, career, collection

   _____

*S*ilken Laumann is Canada's greatest female rower. Her brilliant career and comeback story has been one of Canada's finest moments in sports.

Silken Suzette Laumann was born on November 14, 1964 in Mississauga, Ontario. As a child, Silken admired the accomplishments of Nadia Comaneci, a Russian gymnast, who had received a perfect 10 score in the 1976 Olympics, and hoped one day she would have her own moment of glory. Although Silken's size prevented her from becoming a gymnast, Nadia's passion inspired her to try track and field sports. At the age of 17, with the encouragement of her older sister Danielle, who was a member of the National Rowing Team, Silken decided to try rowing.

Silken's skills in rowing quickly advanced her to a competitive level and in the next two years, she won a gold medal in quadruple sculls at the U.S. Championships, a gold medal in single sculls at the Pan American Games, and at the 1984 Olympics, a bronze medal in the double sculls with her sister Danielle.

Although suffering from back problems and a pinched sciatic nerve, Silken was able to win a second Pan American Games gold medal at the 1987 games in the United States. In the 1990 World Championships, Silken won a silver medal in the single sculls. During the same year, she moved to Victoria, B.C., in order to train year round with former British coach, Mike Spracklin. In 1991, Silken earned a gold at the World Championships in single sculls and became recognized as the new powerhouse in women's rowing. Her success brought her many awards and she was named Canada's Outstanding Athlete of 1991.

Silken was expected to win a gold medal at the 1992 Olympic Games in Barcelonia, Spain. Unfortunately this dream was shattered on May 15, 1992 in Essen, Germany. During a warm up race, Silken's scull was hit broadside by a German double sculls crew. The German scullers and Silken were rowing at full tilt when their sculls collided. Silken's leg took the brunt of the collision. The impact drove a piece of splashboard into Silken's leg. The bone in her leg was fractured, nerves were damaged, and muscles were severely torn. The damage to her leg permanently weakened it. After five operations in a ten day period and a skin graft, doctors announced that Silken's Olympic career was over and that she might not even be able to row for recreation.

During her stay in the hospital, Silken started to do upper body exercises in her bed as she was determined to go to the Olympics. Following a three week stay in the hospital, Silken insisted on being helped from her wheelchair into a racing scull by her husband. For the next five weeks, with the help of a leg brace, Silken trained to get ready for the Barcelona Olympics. Athletes in the world of rowing and spectators could not believe their eyes when they saw her racing. Her race was an astounding feat in the single sculls and her bronze medal was even greater than winning a gold.

During 1993, Silken took the year off from competitive rowing to allow her leg to heal. She used this time to share her story during motivational speaking engagements and co-authored a book entitled *Rowing*.

In the 1996 Olympic Games in Atlanta, Georgia, Silken won a silver medal in the single sculls. This was her final competitive race. Although the Olympic Gold eluded Silken, perhaps she realized "that the most important thing in life is not the winning but the struggle." Today, Silken spends time with her family, doing public speaking, writing, and charity work.

Silken Laumann

Name: _____ Date: _____

Reading Skills

1. Why did Silken Laumann choose rowing as her sport?
_____
_____

2. How do you know Silken adapted to rowing easily?
_____
_____

3. When did Silken become a recognized single sculler?
_____
_____

4. What special award was she given in 1991?
_____
_____

5. How was Silken's Olympic dream shattered?
_____
_____

6. In what ways did Silken display courage and determination after her accident?
_____
_____
_____
_____

7. When and where did Silken compete for the last time and what did she win?
_____
_____
_____

8. Do you agree or disagree with the following statement? Explain why.
" The most important thing in life is not the winning but the struggle."
_____
_____
_____

Vocabulary Skills

A. The words "scull" and "scullers" begins with the "sc" blend. In the word search look for words that begin with the same blend. Circle each one. Then match each word to its meaning below the puzzle. Record the word on the line provided.

```
B A E Z S C A L D O N T K L
D F D A C I E W V X U S M R
F H B G A C T N A C S F H P
A S C A B J E K G B Y D G J
P C B O B D L N H E I Z Q A
Q A W C A V R L M I S J W Y
T F R M R U A K L V C A Z X
P F O S D U C B A C O B D E
R O T N F G S C A L L O P K
B L Q C F G H C I M D J L A
S D F E D I S H D B F I K L
J Q R R S S C A L P G J N M
N K A T U W A X C E H H O P
L S C A P E L Y D S C A R E
M O S P V Z E A B E F G C A
```

B. 1. skin on one's head _____

2. a sword holder _____

3. a kind of seafood _____

4. a surgeon's knife _____

5. very little _____

6. to frighten _____

7. a piece of clothing _____

8. a red colour _____

9. used for weighing _____

10. to discipline _____

11. a dried sore _____

12. used to work up high _____

13. to burn with water _____

SSJ1-77 Famous Female Athletes

*H*urdling is a kind of track and field race. The athlete runs and strides over a structure called a hurdle. Peridita Felicien is a Canadian track and field hurdler. She was born in Oshawa, Ontario on August 29, 1980 and raised in Pickering Ontario.

Perdita began competing in track and field events and started with the 100 meter dash as she was inspired by World and Olympic champions Donovan Bailey and Bruni Surin from Canada. During her high school years at Pineridge Secondary School in Pickering, Perdita dedicated herself to hurdling and won the Ontario High School Hurdling Championship in 1997. This feat earned her the Athlete of the Year award at Pineridge.

In 1998, Perdita was the Ontario High School Champion again and also added the first of two consecutive Canadian Junior Championships. At a scholastic meet in Ohio, her performance brought her offers of athletic scholarships from several American universities. Perdita chose to attend the University of Illinois, where she enrolled in the study of Kinesiology.

During her first year of competing at the university level, Perdita earned All-American honours and set the record for the fastest time by a freshman in NCAA history in the 100 meter hurdles. In the next year, Perdita was ranked number one in the 100 meter hurdles by the NCAA for the entire outdoor season. She became the first Illinois athlete to ever win an indoor and outdoor season national championships. Perdita was the Illinois Female Athlete of the Year for three consecutive years. She was also voted as the National Female Outdoor Athlete of the Year by the U.S. Track Coaches Association.

During 2003, Perdita won her second consecutive 100 meter hurdle national title. She was named the Big Ten Conference "Athlete of the Year" which was a first for a University of Illinois female athlete. In the same year, she was honoured with the title NCAA Female Track and Field Athlete of the Year.

With all these accolades and honours, Perdita became a major force on the international scene for hurdling. In 2003, at the World Championships in Paris, France, Perdita won the 100 meter hurdles final. With this win, she became Canada's first ever female gold medallist and the first female in Illinois

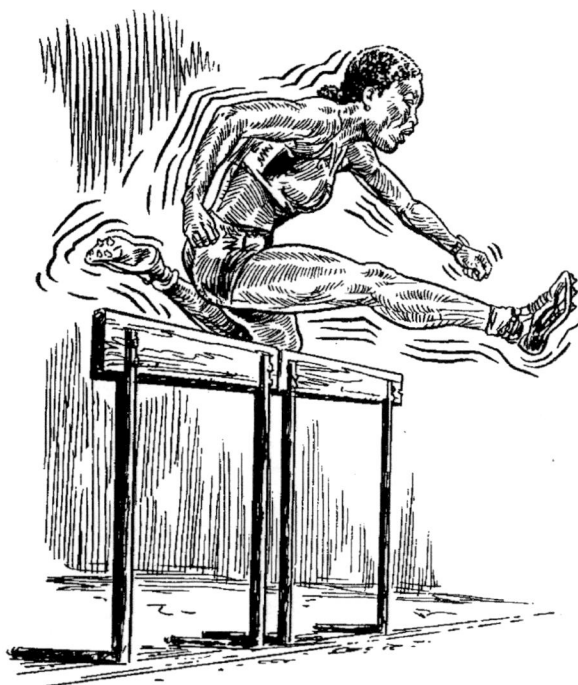

track and field history to win a gold medal in an individual event at the World Championships. Perdita was named Canada's Female Athlete of the Year and was the first track athlete in 25 years to capture this honour.

In March of 2004, Perdita had to go up against the hurdling great Gail Divers at the IAAF World Championships in Budapest, Hungary. She not only beat Gail Divers, but set a new record. After this competition, Perdita won six more hurdling events that lead up to the Summer Olympics in Athens, Greece in 2004.

In the Athens Olympics, Perdita was expected to win gold in the 100 meter hurdles. On August 23, 2004, an unfortunate event took place. Perdita failed to clear the first hurdle and fell into the adjacent lane knocking down the Russian athlete and taking her out of the race as well. Perdita was shocked and devastated after the accident, not only for herself, but for the other athlete as well.

Perdita did return to the track and has had some success winning medals at various events. In 2007, she won a silver medal at the World Championships in the hurdles. In 2008, Perdita did not have the chance to redeem her self-esteem and her reputation in the hurdles at the Olympics in Beijing, as she had to withdraw due to a foot injury. ✪

Perdita Felicien

Name: _____   Date: _____

Reading Skills

Answer each question with a complete sentence.

1. Where and when did Perdita begin competing as a hurdler?
_____
_____

2. What success did Perdita achieve during her high school years?
_____
_____

3. What other Canadian Championship did she win two years in a row?
_____
_____

4. What did her athletic performance bring when she competed in Ohio?
_____
_____

5. Which university did Perdita choose and what did she study?
_____
_____

6. What is Kinesiology and why do you think she chose it to study?
_____
_____

7. Why was Perdita named Canada's Female Athlete of the Year in 2003?
_____
_____

8. Why did Perdita not complete her race in the Athens Olympics?
_____
_____

9. If Perdita had been able to compete at the Beijing Olympics, what thoughts might have crossed her mind before the race?
_____
_____

Vocabulary Skills

A *hurdle* is the structure which a *hurdler* strides over. In the words *hurdle* and *hurdler,* the letters "ur" make the "r" sound. Complete the crossword puzzle with words that have the "ur" sound and match each meaning.

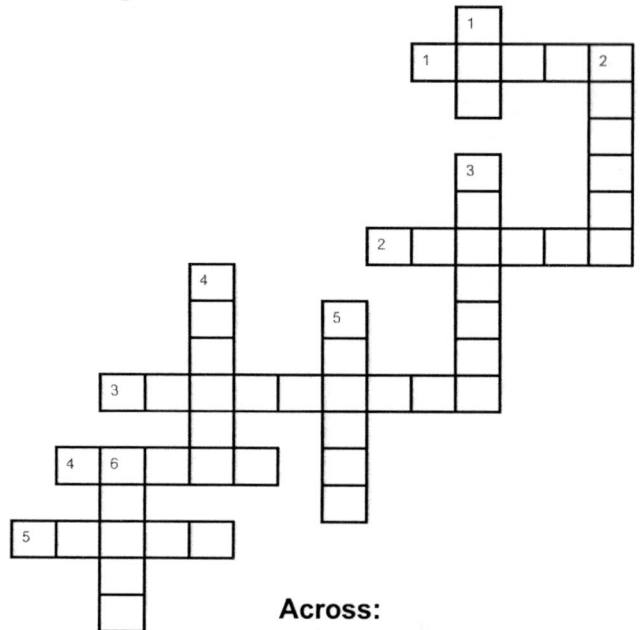

Across:
1. an explosion
2. a dark, rich colour
3. meat in a bun
4. worn by a cowboy
5. works in a hospital

Down:
1. an animal's coat
2. an animal with a shell
3. a thief
4. to talk softly
5. a farm bird
6. used to carry money

Research Skills

Using the Internet or the resource centre, research the sport of hurdling. Find out the skills an athlete would need in order to participate in the sport.

Nancy Greene is well known for her aggressive skiing ability that earned her the nickname Tiger, while skiing the various slopes around the world. She has won more medals than any other Canadian skier and was named the greatest Canadian female athlete of the twentieth century. Nancy grew up in a family that loved to ski and lived in a mountainous community called Rossland in British Columbia. Nancy and her siblings began skiing at the age of three. During high school, Nancy began ski racing and in 1958, she won her first trophy, placing second to her older sister Elizabeth in the Canadian Junior Championships.

In 1958, Nancy also made the Canadian team for the Squaw Valley Olympics to be held in the United States in 1960. In order to compete with the world's best, Nancy practised and refined her skiing skills and style. During her first Olympics, at the age of 16, her results showed great promise, but Nancy was not satisfied. She had placed 22nd in the downhill, 26th in the giant slalom and 31st in the slalom. During the games, Nancy roomed with Anne Heggtveit from Ottawa, who won the gold medal in the slalom for Canada. Anne's win gave Nancy the determination to win a gold medal at the Olympics.

For the next few years, Nancy honed her skiing skills in readiness for the next Olympics, which were to be held in Innsbruck, Austria. However, when Nancy competed at these games, she found herself in 7th place in the downhill, 15th place in the slalom, and 16th place in the giant slalom. Nancy returned home very dejected and frustrated. She realized that she wasn't quite ready to win a gold medal and knew that she also needed more involvement in competitions with international skiers. She brought this problem to the attention of the officials of the Canadian skiing program: they agreed and her wish was granted. Canadian skiers would become more involved in competitive international sports. At the same time, the World Cup was created for elite downhill skiers.

During Nancy's racing career, she won three United States Championship titles and nine Canadian titles. In 1967, she won the first overall skiing title in the first World Cup with a victory of 1/100th of a second in the last race of the year, defeating a strong French ski team.

In preparation for the 1968 Olympics to be held in Grenoble, France, Nancy trained on the slopes in the area. A month before the games, she slipped during a training run and wiped out. The ligaments in her right ankle were badly pulled. Nancy was optimistic and let physiotherapy repair the injury as she knew all of her skiing skills were ready.

During her first race, which was the downhill, she came in tenth place. Her fans wondered if she was really ready. In the slalom, Nancy whisked down the course in one minute, 26.15 seconds winning the silver medal. Canadians were thrilled, but Nancy still wanted that top spot on the podium. On February 15, Nancy's final chance for golden glory came in the giant slalom. She was the ninth skier out of the gate and attacked the course at a blistering pace, making her turns precisely in order to save time. When she crossed the finish line, her time did not light up on the scoreboard. For several anxious minutes, Nancy waited for her time to show and when it did she realized she had beaten the leader by 2.64 seconds and she had won the medal that had been alluding her - GOLD!

At the end of the 1968 season, Nancy retired from competitive skiing, going out at the top of the world at just 24 years of age. Nancy Greene is considered the greatest sportswoman that Canada has ever produced. ✪

Nancy Greene

Name: _____   Date: _____

Reading Skills

Answer each question using a word or a few words from the biography.

1. At what age did Nancy begin to ski?
   _____

2. In what year did Nancy win her first skiing trophy?
   _____

3. In which Olympics did Nancy win a silver and gold medal?
   _____

4. Which athlete inspired Nancy to ski for a gold medal?
   _____

5. In which Olympics did Nancy have her worst results?
   _____

6. Which Olympics made Nancy feel dejected and frustrated?
   _____

7. What did Nancy feel Canadian skiers needed?
   _____

8. How many Canadian and American titles did Nancy win altogether?
   _____

9. On what date did Nancy Greene finally achieve her ultimate goal?
   _____

10. Why was Nancy nicknamed Tiger?
   _____

11. When did Nancy injure her right ankle?
   _____

12. Why didn't Nancy know the results of her last race in the Grenoble Olympics when she finished?
   _____

Vocabulary Skills

A. Locate synonyms in the biography for the following words. Record the words on the lines provided.

1. hillsides _____
2. prize _____
3. best _____
4. happy _____
5. last _____
6. very fast _____
7. escaping _____
8. beating _____
9. standings _____
10. speed _____
11. fix _____
12. opportunity _____

B. Name the underlined part of speech in each sentence. Record its name on the line provided.

> Noun, Verb, Adverb, Adjective,
> Phrase, Preposition

1. <u>attacked</u> the course _____
2. <u>in the downhill</u> _____
3. in the <u>United States</u> _____
4. in a <u>mountainous</u> community _____
5. the ninth <u>skier</u> _____
6. were <u>badly</u> pulled _____
7. <u>whisked</u> down the course _____
8. <u>crossed</u> the finish line _____
9. in the <u>last</u> race _____
10. <u>at</u> the age _____

*B*eckie Scott is an elite cross-country skier who blazed a trail for fellow Canadian skiers on a brilliant mid-winter day in 2002 at Soldier Hollow, Utah, capturing the bronze medal in the pursuit race at the Salt Lake City Olympics.

Beckie was born on August 1,1974, in Vegreville, Alberta, and grew up in Vermilion, a small Albertan community. She began cross-country skiing at the age of five. Beckie was an active child and also participated in activities such as dancing, piano, gymnastics, and swimming. Her first competitive sport was swimming but eventually skiing became her primary interest. At the age of seven, she participated in her first cross-country skiing competition.

When Beckie was 13, a new cross-country skiing coach, Len Parsons, moved to Vermilion and she began to take up skiing seriously. Parsons taught her to think big and to believe in herself. In 1988, on her first trip to the Junior National Championships, Beckie realized she had potential and enjoyed the taste of high level competition. It was then that her Olympic dream began to take shape.

The way to the top was not easy, but long and gradual, and some people wondered if her goals and dreams were realistic. Beckie believed in herself and was determined to succeed.

In 1998, at her first Olympic Games in Nagano, Japan, Beckie's best placing was 45th. In 2002, at the Salt Lake City Olympic Games, in Utah, Beckie met with great success. At Soldier Hollow, Utah, the site of the cross-country skiing events, Beckie won a bronze medal in the pursuit race. She became the first Canadian and North American woman to stand on the Olympic podium in cross-country skiing.

Beckie's moment of glory did not end on that day. Two women skiers, who had finished before her, had tested positive for performance enhancing drugs in other races. Beckie believed strongly in honesty and fair play and along with the Canadian Olympic Committee, fought to have both skiers disqualified.

In June of 2003, Beckie was presented with the silver medal that had been taken away from one of the skiers. Months later, the second skier was disqualified and Becky received the gold medal, two and a half years after the Salt Lake City Olympics. Her lengthy battle, due to her strong convictions and belief in fair play, made her a legend in the sporting world.

At the Olympics in Torino, Italy, in February 2006, Beckie and her teammate Sara Renner won a silver medal in the team sprint. During her competitive years, Beckie also captured 15 World Cup medals.

In recognition of her efforts in cross-country skiing, Beckie has been given a variety of awards in Canada and has been inducted into the Alberta Sports Hall of Fame and Canada's Hall of Fame. Beckie is a strong advocate of athletes performing drug free and helped to circulate an athletes' petition requesting the establishment of an independent drug-testing body for all World Cup and Olympic Competitions. She is also known for her support of various charities and was named a UNICEF Canada representative. At one World Cup, she challenged her fellow athletes to donate their winnings to an Afganistan relief project.

Beckie is now happily married and living in Bend, Oregon. She spends her leisure time reading, writing, and cooking. Now she puts on her cross-country skis for fun. ✪

Beckie Scott

Name: _____   Date: _____

Reading Skills

Tell when each of the following events took place in Beckie Scott's life and career.

1. Beckie began to take cross-country skiing seriously.

   _____

2. Sara Renner and Beckie Scott won the silver medal in the team sprint.

   _____

3. Beckie Scott began skiing.

   _____

4. In the pursuit race, Beckie Scott won a bronze medal.

   _____

5. Becky found out she really enjoyed competing.

   _____

6. Beckie's best placing in a race was 45th.

   _____

7. Becky was given the gold medal that she had fought for and deserved.

   _____

8. Beckie Scott was the first Canadian woman cross-country skier to stand on an Olympic podium.

   _____

9. The silver medal was presented to Beckie.

   _____

10. Beckie Scott participated in her first skiing competition.

    _____

Vocabulary Skills

A. Read each clue below. Unscramble the bold letters beside it to find the word that matches the clue and record it on the line provided.

1. a synonym for bright   **allibirtn** _____

2. an antonym for lazy   **eitvca** _____

3. a synonym for skills   **otpneltia** _____

4. an antonym for fail   **decsuce** _____

5. a homonym for fare   **rfia** _____

6. an antonym for negative   **tepoivsi** _____

7. a synonym for give   **teadno** _____

8. a homonym for made   **diam** _____

B. Explain the meaning of each group of words in your own words on the lines provided.

1. blazed a trail _____

   _____

2. capturing the bronze medal _____

   _____

3. her primary interest _____

   _____

4. enjoyed the taste of competition _____

   _____

Research Skills

Using the Internet, research cross-country ski racing to find out the answers to the following questions.

1. What are the types of races held at a cross-country competition?

2. What kind of equipment is used by a cross-country skier?

3. What are some problems a cross-country skier might encounter during a race?

*A*bigail Hoffman was one of Canada's greatest female track and field athletes. She competed in four Olympiads and was Canada's flag-bearer at the 1976 games. Abby was born in Toronto on February 11, 1947. At the age of three, she learned how to skate and had played hockey with her brothers from the age of five. Abby developed great hockey skills and wanted to play on a team. Unfortunately, for Abby, there were no leagues for girls in the Toronto area. Abby decided to cut her hair short and registered her name as "Ab Hoffman" in the boys' league. No one knew she was a girl as she looked very much like a young boy.

Abby played for a St. Catherines, Ontario boys' Junior A hockey league, as a defenceman. All went well for her until she was selected for the all-star team and had to show her birth certificate, which revealed her true gender. Once her secret was known, she was thrust into the spotlight as her story was told in the newspapers, on the radio, and on television.

Even though Abby was disqualified because girls were not allowed to play hockey with boys, she had made her point. This early experience, of seeing the limitations placed on females who wanted to participate in male-dominated sports, helped her later when she worked at the Ontario Human Rights Commission and at Sports Canada.

Abby gave up organized sports and tried others such as swimming and track and field. It was track and field in which Abby found her place and the 800 meter event became her specialty as a middle-distance runner. For a number of years, Abbey belonged to an all-male club and struggled for acceptance as an athlete. By the mid 1960's, she became one of Canada's top athletes.

Abby won eight Canadian national titles in the 800 meter and held the national record from 1962-1975. At the Commonwealth Games in 1966, Abby captured the gold medal in the 880 yard event. She won bronze in the 800 meter at the World

University Games in 1965 and silver in 1967. In 1969, at the Maccabiah Games, Abby struck gold in the 400 meter and the 800 meter. In 1971, at the Pan American Games, she won gold in the 800 meter and bronze in both the 800 meter and 1,500 meter races at the 1967 and 1975 competitions.

Abby Hoffman represented Canada in four Olympic Games and in 1976, she proudly carried the Canadian flag and led the team into Montreal's Olympic Stadium during the opening ceremonies for her last competition. Although Abby's competitive career ended at the Montreal Games, she has remained a strong force in the Canadian Olympic movement. Abby was the first woman elected to the executive of the Canadian Olympic Association, as Director General of Sport Canada in 1981. She has been a leader in gaining recognition for high performance female athletes at university, national, and international levels.

For all of her work and effort, Abby has been awarded the Ontario Award of Merit (1975), City of Toronto Civic Award of Merit (1976), and the Order of Canada (1982). Many women compete today in sports that were once male-dominated, thanks to Abby Hoffman's efforts over the years. ✪

Abigail (Abby) Hoffman

Name: _____   Date: _____

Reading Skills

Answer each question with a complete sentence.

1. Why did Abbey play on a boys' hockey team?
   _____
   _____

2. How did Abby fool the hockey league she played in?
   _____
   _____

3. When did Abby's gender get discovered?
   _____
   _____

4. Why do you think girls are not allowed to play on boys' hockey teams?
   _____
   _____

5. Do you think that girls should have the opportunity to play the sport of their choice?
   _____
   _____

6. Which sport did Abby Hoffman choose to compete in?
   _____
   _____

7. Why is Abby considered one of Canada's greatest female athletes?
   _____
   _____
   _____

8. How has Abby Hoffman improved sports for female athletes?
   _____
   _____
   _____

Vocabulary Skills

A. On the line provided, record the base word for each of the following words.

1. competed _____
2. unfortunately _____
3. disqualified _____
4. limitations _____
5. speciality _____
6. acceptance _____
7. ceremonies _____
8. international _____

B. Use each group of words in a sentence about Abby Hoffman.

1. flag-bearer, ceremonies, Olympics
   _____
   _____

2. newspaper, girl, hockey
   _____
   _____

3. specialty, event, track and field
   _____
   _____

4. bronze, meter, games
   _____
   _____

5. believed, fairness, athletes
   _____
   _____

C. Create three questions that you would ask Abby Hoffman during an interview.
   _____
   _____
   _____
   _____
   _____
   _____
   _____
   _____

*H*ayley Wickenheiser is considered the greatest female hockey player in the world. In 2003, Hayley was the first female player to score a point in a men's professional game when she played in the Finnish hockey league. Hayley was named the MVP of Canada's gold medal-winning team at both the 2002 Salt Lake City and 2006 Torino Winter Olympics. Her talent is unsurpassed.

Hayley Wickenheiser was born on August 12, 1978, in Shaunavon, Saskatchewan and is the oldest of three children. She learned to skate on a backyard rink, created by her parents, at the age of six. On this rink is where Hayley's love for hockey began. As a youngster, she played on a local boys' team and was the only girl. On many occasions, Hayley had to put on her gear in boiler rooms and other places in rinks as there often wasn't any available dressing rooms. It was a fight for her to enroll in a hockey school in Swift Current where, again, she was the only girl. Finally, her family moved to Calgary, Alberta so that she could play on an all-girls' team in the city. Hayley was a member of Team Alberta in the Canada Winter Games for the Under-17 Girls' Competition in 1991. At the competition, she helped her team to win a gold medal by scoring the winning goal and was named the MVP of the final game.

In 1994, at the age of 15, Hayley was chosen to play on Canada's National Women's Team. Her teammates who were much older nicknamed her "Highchair Hayley" because she was so young. During her first international tournament, at the 1994 World Championships in Lake Placid, her team won gold. In 1997, at her second World Championships her team captured the gold medal again and Hayley earned a spot on the tournament All-Star Team, which was the first of four times for her to be chosen. In 1999, Hayley helped Canada to win another gold medal and became the tournament MVP. Hayley has six World Championship gold medals and two silver medals. In 2001, she was named to play on Team Canada but had an injury and couldn't participate.

Hayley was a member of Team Canada at the 1998 Winter Olympics. This was the first time women's hockey was introduced as a sport. Canada won a silver medal and Hayley was named to the tournament all-star team.

In 2002, Hayley made the roster again for Team Canada and played in the Winter Olympics held in Salt Lake City, Utah. This time, Team Canada beat the United States in the final game and won the gold. In the Torino Olympics in Italy, Canada was defending its gold medal status against Sweden, a surprise finalist, and won. Hayley was named MVP, Top Forward, and awarded a place on the all-star team.

During her hockey career, Hayley continued her studies at the University of Calgary in its pre-med program. In 2000, she qualified for a spot on the Canadian womens' softball team and travelled to the 2000 Summer Olympics in Sydney, Australia. She was the second Canadian woman to ever compete in both Winter and Summer Olympics.

When Hayley finished her amateur hockey career, she began to play on professional hockey teams. She chose to play on European teams as the game is played more openly and is less physical. For a brief period of time, Hayley played on a team for Finland and then signed a contract to play for a Swedish men's league.

Hayley has always advised young hockey players to work hard, think smart, and to give no excuses in their sport. She has been an excellent role model and an athlete to admire. ✪

Hayley Wickenheiser

Name: _____   Date: _____

Reading Skills

Number the events that have taken place in Hayley Wickenheiser's life in the correct order.

_____ Since it was difficult for Hayley to play on an all-girl team, her family moved to the city of Calgary.

_____ Hayley had to play on a boys' hockey team as there was no girls' team in the area.

_____ In Shaunavon, Saskatchewan, on August 12, 1978, the Wickenheiser's welcomed a baby girl into their family and named her Hayley.

_____ Hayley eventually turned professional and played hockey on European teams.

_____ At Lake Placid, Hayley played in her first international competition, the 1994 World Championship, where her team won gold.

_____ Hayley began playing hockey on her backyard rink, at the age of six.

_____ In 1994, Hayley was picked to play on Canada's National Women's Team, at the age of 15.

_____ Hayley was named MVP and Top Forward when Canada won the gold at the Torino Olympics in Italy in 2006.

_____ In 1991, Hayley scored the winning goal at the Canada Winter Games for the Under-17 Girls' Competition and her team won a gold medal.

_____ At the Salt Lake City Olympics, Hayley played on Team Canada when they won gold by defeating the United States.

Vocabulary Skills

A. Classify each group of words as antonyms (A), synonyms (S), and homonyms (H) on the line provided.

1. professional, amateur _____

2. brief, short _____

3. for, against _____

4. tournament, competition _____

5. currant, current _____

6. team, teem _____

7. won, beat _____

8. winning, losing _____

9. talent, ability _____

10. gear, equipment _____

B. Record the correct homonym in each sentence.

role, roll	beat, beet	time, thyme
team, teem	been, bean	

1. Her _____ in the play was quite funny.

2. Team Canada _____ Team U.S.A. at the Salt Lake City Olympics.

3. My mother used some _____ to make her stew taste better.

4. Which _____ did you want to win gold at the Olympics?

5. The _____ that he planted grew into a huge plant.

6. Suddenly, the rain began to _____ down and we had to run fast to our car.

7. The boy pulled a large red _____ out of the garden.

8. "Where have you _____ all this time?" asked the boy's mother.

9. I watched as the ball began to _____ under the bed.

10. The old man checked the clock for the _____.

Marnie McBean and Kathleen Heddle were scullers who dominated the world rowing scene in the 1990's and became the first Canadians to win three Summer Olympic gold medals. As partners, they raced in the eights, straight pairs, double sculls and in quad sculls.

Marnie McBean was born in Vancouver, British Columbia on January 28, 1968 and was raised in Toronto, Ontario. She was introduced to rowing at the Argonaut Rowing Club and a year later, showed great potential at the World Junior Rowing Championships.

Kathleen Heddle was born in Trail, British Columbia on November 27, 1965 and was raised in Vancouver. While growing up, she tried to match or achieve the same results that her older sisters had done in various sports. While attending the University of British Columbia, Kathleen discovered rowing and began competing and winning medals on the varsity rowing team. In 1987, Heddle joined the national team and won gold in the pair event at the Pan American Games.

In 1991, McBean and Heddle teamed up for the first time. Their partnership was often referred to as the "odd couple" as both women were as different as day and night in personality. Heddle was quiet, shy and very much an introvert, while McBean was agile, quick and changeable. Together, they formed an outstanding rowing team.

In McBean and Heddle's first race, the Canadian pair beat the defending world champions in 1991. Later in the same year, the combo won gold at the World Championships and were also part of the eights crew that finished first. In 1992, the duo repeated their world championship success at the Barcelona Olympics by winning gold in both the pairs and eights. After this win, their lives changed drastically. When they returned home from the Olympics, they realized they had done something impressive by the attention they received from the media and their fans.

When 1996 rolled around, the pressure was on McBean and Heddle as they were again the World Champions heading into the Olympic

Games at Atlanta, Georgia in the United States. It was difficult to stay focused due to all the media attention before the games, but they managed to keep on track with their training. At the games, the pair won gold in double sculls and earned a bronze in quadruple sculls.

A year later, McBean and Heddle were inducted into the Canadian Sports Hall of Fame. Heddle decided to give up racing and retired to start a family. McBean still wanted to compete and set her sights on the next Olympics in Sydney, Australia. At the 2000 Olympics, McBean was sent to represent Canada in the single sculls and it was here that she hoped to win her fourth gold medal. McBean did qualify in the single sculls but unfortunately she was not the favourite to win. A few days before the race, a back injury forced her to withdraw from the competition. McBean was very disappointed with the missed opportunity, but realized it was a gift in the end as she had the time to sit back and evaluate the Olympics without blinders on and listen to comments and conversations made by the Canadian team.

McBean and Heddle won many medals during their rowing careers and have been honoured with a variety of awards. They each have helped young rowers train and prepare for competitions. They are well respected Canadian athletes and excellent role models. ✪

Marnie McBean and Kathleen Heddle

Name: _____   Date: _____

Reading Skills

Record the correct name(s) on the line in each sentence.

McBean or **Heddle** or **McBean and Heddle**

1. _____ raced in the World Junior Rowing Championships.

2. _____ beat the defending world champions in 1991.

3. _____ gave up rowing and retired to begin a family.

4. _____ won gold at the Barcelona Olympics in the pairs and the eights.

5. _____ began rowing at the Argonaut Rowing Club in Toronto.

6. At the Atlanta Olympic Games, _____ won gold in double sculls and a bronze in quadruple sculls.

7. While at university, _____ began rowing and competing on the varsity rowing team.

8. _____ wanted to keep rowing and competing and began training for the Sydney Olympic Games in Australia

9. _____ did not win the fourth medal that she hoped for at the Sydney Olympics.

10. _____ made an awesome rowing team even though they were complete opposites in personality.

11. _____ had a lively, out-going personality and was inclined to make quick decisions.

12. _____ was shy and quiet and knew how to calm her teammate.

Vocabulary Skills

A. The word quadruple begins with the blend "qu" and it means having four parts. Record each "qu" word beside its meaning on the line provided.

quantity	quarrel	quarry
quench	quaint	quail
quake	quality	queer
quirk	quiz	quest

1. a place where stone is dug _____

2. a quick test _____

3. an amount or portion _____

4. to put an end to _____

5. an angry disagreement _____

6. strange or odd in an amusing or interesting way _____

7. nature, kind, or character of something ____ _____

8. a plump game bird _____

9. strange, odd, different _____

10. a search or hunt for something _____

11. a strange way of acting _____

12. to tremble or shake _____

B. Use the following homophones in sentences to illustrate their meanings.

1. skull: _____
   _____
   scull: _____
   _____

2. due: _____
   _____
   dew: _____
   _____
   do: _____
   _____

*C*atriona Le May Doan is considered one of the fastest women to fly around a track on ice skates. She held the World Record in the 500 meter for ten years and has broken 8 world records during her career. Catriona has been a world champion and an Olympic champion as well.

Catriona was born and raised in Saskatoon, Saskatchewan and is the youngest of three girls. Being a natural athlete, she was involved in a variety of sports such as soccer, track and field, and ringette at an early age. Catriona began speed skating when she was ten and loved the sport because it was different and exciting. In 1983, at 13, Catriona competed in the Canada Winter Games and won a medal in short-track speed skating. In 1987, she returned to win a silver and a bronze. At the Canada Summer Games, Catriona competed as a hurdler and is one of a few Canadians to have competed in Canada's Winter and Summer Games.

Speed skating became her passion and she made her Olympic debut at the Albertville Winter Olympics, finishing 14th in the 500 meter and 31st in the 1000 meter, which was not a bad start. In 1994, at the Lillehammer Olympics Games disaster stuck. Catriona fell during the 500 meter race and she finished 33rd. The fall devastated and depressed Catriona and she lost her self-confidence. It took her months before she could bring herself to put on her skates and train. Finally, after being encouraged by friends, family, teammates, and her future husband, Catriona began training again.

On November 22, 1997, Catriona was the woman to break the 38 seconds barrier for the 500 meter race while skating in Calgary, Alberta. Her time was 37.90 seconds. Before the year was over, she had tied her record once and broken it twice, ending with a record time of 37.55 seconds. During the next four years, Catriona broke her record four more times, ending with the time of 37.22 seconds in Calgary in December of 2001. No other woman has set eight consecutive World Records in one distance.

In 1998, at the Nagano Winter Olympics, in Japan, Catriona won the Olympic 500 meter gold medal and the bronze medal in the 1000 meter. In 2002, at the Salt Lake City Olympics Games in Utah, Catriona repeated this feat in the 500 meter race and was called "the fastest woman on ice".

During Catriona's career, she has been World Sprint Champion in 1998 and 2002 as well as World Champion in the 500 meter race in 1998, 1999, and 2001. In 2000, she won a bronze medal in the 500 meter race. During the years 1998, 1999, 2001, and 2002, Catriona won the 500 meter World Cup four years consecutively. In 1998, she won the 1000 meter race in the World Cup as well.

Catriona's accomplishments earned her the Lou Marsh Award as Canada's Athlete of the Year in 2002. Three times she has been the recipient of this award. Catriona remains involved in sports as a motivational speaker, serves on various Olympic committees, and is often seen on television hosting sporting events. She has received three Honorary Degrees from the University of Calgary, the University of Saskatchewan, and the University of Regina. Catriona has been inducted into Canada's Hall of Fame and the Canadian Olympic Committee's Sports Hall of Fame, and appointed an Officer of the Order of Canada. ✪

Catriona Le May Doan

Name: _____   Date: _____

Reading Skills

On the line at the end of each sentence, record true or false on the line provided.

1. Catriona Le May Doan is a speed skater who excelled at racing in the 1000 meter race. _____

2. Catriona is an Olympic and World champion athlete. _____

3. Le May Doan grew up with two sisters in Winnipeg, Manitoba. _____

4. A terrible collision with other speed skaters caused Catriona to lose her self-confidence. _____

5. Catriona is the only woman who has ever set eight consecutive World Records in the 500 meter race. _____

6. Catriona chose speed skating as a sport because it was fast and exciting. _____

7. During her career, Catriona has broken ten world records in the 1000 meter race. _____

8. Catriona won a medal in every Olympic Games in which she participated. _____

9. Catriona won the 500 meter race at the World Cup four years in a row. _____

10. Catriona holds the record for the fastest time in the 500 meter race. _____

11. Catriona has competed in the summer and winter games as a speed skater. _____

12. Her first Olympic competition was at the Albertville Winter Olympics. _____

Vocabulary Skills

Catriona was a speed skater. The word skater begins with the blend "sk". Circle the words in the word search that begin with the same blend and match each meaning. Record the word beside its meaning.

```
R Z E S H Y S K E P T I C A L
A S K I N F U M M V L K H W U
C K A D Q N P G Q T I R C J X
O A B B T P V S N S K I T J S
K T J L L C O K P L A O E L K
L E T M L R Q E N O K M K Z Y
I B H M U P D I U W O B S H X
T O S G K S F N E V A P N Q J
N A O R S Q N C L F B O I G H
P R U R D K M I Z Y T G C X S
Q D R V S Z N J L E W H J R K
G T U S W E L Y L M E K D G U
V H U W X U V E X T Y I Z S N
W V K T X C K Z H S K A T F K
F X W J Y S F B C A N C E A F
I E Y D Z Q A B O P C D E D B
```

1. a card game for three players _____

2. a narrow board on wheels _____

3. coiled bundle of yarn _____

4. the bones of a body _____

5. doubting, not believing easily _____

6. a rough, quickly drawn picture _____

7. a body's covering _____

8. a short play _____

9. bones of the head _____

10. a smelly animal _____

In the late 1960's and much of the 1970's, Beverly Boys, a young woman from Toronto, led the way in the Canadian diving world. She became famous for her ability to execute precise dives from the 10 meter tower and the 3 meter springboard. Beverly dominated Canadian and international meets for about 10 years. During her career, she won 34 Canadian championships as well as many international titles.

At the Commonwealth Games, Beverly won medals easily. At the Games in Scotland, in 1970, she came home with two gold medals and from the games in New Zealand in 1974, Beverly won a gold as well. During the Pan American Games in 1967 and 1971, Beverly won a total of three medals - two silver and a bronze.

As a world-class diver, Beverly competed in three Olympic Games representing Canada. Her best showing was at the Mexico City Olympics. She had not performed well during the finals and was sitting in 19th place. Beverly knew that in order to impress the judges and to improve her standing, she must make this dive her very best in the 10 meter event.

Standing at the top of the tower, Beverly decided to use her best dive, which was a one and a-half somersault with a triple twist. This dive had a 2.9 degree of difficulty. Her dive was flawless with very little splash as she entered the water. This dive bumped her up to fourth place ranking. This was the highest mark ever awarded to a Canadian female diver at that time. For her achievements in diving, Beverly was awarded the Bobbie Rosenfield Trophy as Canada's Top Female Athlete in 1968 and 1969.

Sylvie Bernier became interested in the sport of diving when she watched her brother during his diving lessons. She took to diving readily and at the age of 11, had won her first regional championship. At the age of 14, Sylvie became a member of the national diving team and soon became a champion in the 3 meter springboard event.

Sylvie soon became a regular competitor to stand on an international podium. During her six year diving career, she has won more than 20 medals. At the 1982 Commonwealth Games she won a silver medal, at the Pan-American Games a bronze, and at the 1983 World University Games another bronze.

Sylvie's best year took place in 1984, when she came first in three major competitions - the Canadian Championships, Dive Canada, and the Fort Lauderdale International in Florida. This was a phenomenal lead up to the 1984 Olympic Games in Los Angeles, California. Expectations were very high and the pressure was on Sylvie, but she did not disappoint her country and her supporters. Sylvie's spectacular performance during the 3 meter springboard event earned her a gold medal. This was Canada's first Olympic gold medal in diving. As well as winning a medal, Sylvie also set an Olympic record with her score of 530.70.

Her remarkable achievements earned her the Bobbie Rosenfeld award as Canada's Female Athlete of the Year as well as the Elaine Tanner Trophy as Canada's Junior Female Athlete of the Year. Sylvie was Quebec's first Female Olympic Champion and received the Order of Quebec as well as the Order of Canada. She was the first diver to be honoured by the International Swimming Hall of Fame. ✪

Beverly Boys and Sylvie Bernier

Name: _____   Date: _____

Reading Skills

Each of the following statements describes a Canadian diver. Record the correct diver's name on the line provided.

Is it Beverly Boys or Sylvie Bernier?

1. Her incredibly clean dive, with very little splash, bumped her up fifteen places in the Olympic competition. _____

2. She won her first championship at the age of 11. _____

3. In order to be a ten meter tower diver, this athlete could not be afraid of heights. _____

4. As a diver, she dominated the Canadian and international competitions for many years. _____

5. She became a member of the national diving team when she was only 14 years old. _____

6. This Canadian diver competed in the 3 meter springboard as well as the 10 meter tower. _____

7. During her six year diving career, she collected more than 20 medals. _____

8. She won the Bobbie Rosenfeld Trophy twice._____

9. Canada's first gold medal in Olympic diving was won by this athlete. _____

10. She competed in the Olympics three times, but never won a medal. _____

11. Her diving score set an Olympic record. _____

12. Her best dive was a one and a-half somersault with a triple twist. _____

Vocabulary Skills

Copy the following paragraph on the lines provided. Capitalize and punctuate in all the necessary places in order to make it a complete paragraph.

beverly boys and sylvie bernier were famous canadian female divers they both competed in the olympic games the commonwealth games and were canadian champions beverly boys dove from the 10 meter tower and the 3 meter springboard while sylvie bernier only competed on the 3 meter springboard both divers each won many different coloured medals but sylvie was the only one to bring home an olympic gold medal in diving both divers were honoured with the bobbie rosenfeld award.

_____
_____
_____
_____
_____
_____
_____
_____
_____
_____
_____
_____
_____
_____
_____

Research Skills

Using the Internet, research to find out the names of the different types of dives that a diver must be able to do in order to compete at competitions.

Vicki Keith was not considered an athletic child during her school years and was usually the last to be picked for teams. Fortunately, Vicki refused to accept the negative comments about her abilities and maintained a positive attitude about herself. As a result, Vicki became the most successful marathon swimmer in the history of the sport and holds sixteen world records.

Her marathon swimming career began in Kingston, Ontario, in August of 1985, with her world-record crossing of Lake Ontario using the butterfly stroke. In 1998, Vicki became the first person to cross all five Great Lakes and had swam Lake Ontario a record of 5 times, including a double crossing of 104 km. Vicki swam 22 km around Sydney Harbour in May of 1989, and in July of the same year, swam 33.7 km across the English Channel. In August of 1989, Vicki swam 32 km across the Juan de Fuca Strait and 28 km across Lake Winnipeg. During September of 1989, she crossed Lake Ontario and the 35 km Catalina Channel. Vicki has also participated in pool marathons. In October of 1985, she set a record of 100 hours in a continuous pool swim and in June of 1996, she broke her own record by swimming 129 hours and 45 minutes in a pool.

Many of Vicki's marathon swims were completed to raise awareness, as well as money, for disabled children. Her swims raised more than $800,000.00 for Variety Clubs worldwide. Some of this money helped to build the Variety Village Sunshine Pool in Toronto.

When Vicki retired from competition marathons, she focussed her attention on coaching a competitive swimming team of athletes with physical disabilities at Variety Village. She believed that disabled athletes should be able to compete at swim meets with able-bodied athletes. Vickie noticed that there were very few swimming meets for disabled athletes and many for able-bodied swimmers. She began to push various committees to allow her athletes with disabilities to compete at the same meets as regular athletes. The committees agreed and today this is an accepted happening at swimming meets. Swimming is the most integrated of all the sports in Canada at the provincial and national levels.

During Vicki's coaching career, she has coached seven athletes with a disability to the national level and three athletes with a disability in marathon swimming. Carlos Costa, a double leg amputee, became the first athlete with a disability to swim across Lake Ontario. Ashley Cowan, a quadruple amputee swam across Lake Erie and Terri-Lynn Langdon who has Cerebral Palsy swam the 20 km across Lake Erie.

In 2001, when Vicki moved back to Kingston, she began a swim team for young people with physical disabilities at the Kingston Family YMCA called the Kingston Y Penguins. When the YMCA needed financial assistance for new programs for disabled children, Vicki came out of retirement to complete another marathon swim of 63 hours and 40 minutes in Lake Ontario and completed 80.2 km using her famous butterfly stroke. She raised over two hundred thousand dollars for the Family YMCA, which brought her lifetime fund raising total to over one million dollars.

For all of her work and efforts, Vicki has been made a member of the Order of Canada, inducted into the Terry Fox Hall of Fame and had her famous arrival and departure points in Toronto renamed after her. The Leslie Street Spit is now called the Vicki Keith Point. ✪

Vicki Keith

Name: _____   Date: _____

Reading Skills

Complete the following activities.

1. What is a marathon swimmer?
   _____
   _____

2. Vicki Keith is a famous Canadian marathon swimmer. What characteristics would an athlete have to have in order to be a successful marathon swimmer?
   _____
   _____
   _____
   _____

3. What are some of the risks a marathon swimmer might experience during a marathon swim?
   _____
   _____
   _____
   _____

4. List the names of the types of bodies of waters a marathon swimmer might swim?
   _____
   _____

5. In what ways was Vicki Keith an amazing marathon swimmer?
   _____
   _____
   _____
   _____

6. How has Vicki Keith improved the life and self-esteem of disabled children?
   _____
   _____
   _____
   _____

Vocabulary Skills

A. On the line beside each word, record its base word.

1. abilities _____
2. swimmer _____
3. continuous _____
4. assistance _____
5. disabled _____
6. arrival _____
7. provincial _____
8. awareness _____

B. Skim through the biography to find four compound words. Record them on the lines provided.

   _____
   _____
   _____
   _____

C. Divide each of the following words into syllables on the line provided.

1. disabilities _____
2. fortunately _____
3. swimming _____
4. participated _____
5. amputee _____
6. departure _____
7. integrated _____
8. disabled _____

D. Use the following homophones in sentences to show their meanings.

1. straight: _____
   _____

2. strait: _____
   _____

Synchronized swimming is often referred to as water ballet. It is a sport that requires athletic ability, precise performance, and communication. While working with a partner, a swimmer must be able to communicate, while at the same time perform with technical precision. Two of Canada's famous synchro swimmers had these skills and the uncanny ability to understand each other above or below the water. Michelle Cameron and Carolyn Waldo are Canada's most successful synchronized swimming duo.

Carolyn Waldo was born and raised in Montreal, Quebec. When she was three years old, she nearly drowned and it took several years for her to get over fear of the water but when she did, she was able to master the skills of synchronised swimming. At the age of 11, in 1975, Carolyn began her competitive synchro career. At the age of 15, she became a national team member. Six times Carolyn was a World Champion as a solo synchro swimmer and at the age of 20, she won a silver medal at the 1984 Olympic Games.

Michelle Cameron's hometown is Calgary, Alberta and she took up competitive synchronised swimming in 1976, at the age of 14. She swam with her hometown club called the Aquabelles. The Aquabelles won six of eight national championships between 1981 and 1988. They were coached by Debbie Muir, who had a great reputation of coaching winning synchro teams.

In 1982, Carolyn Waldo decided to join the Aquabelles so she could be coached by Debbie Muir. Muir recognized that Carolyn and Michelle had similar attributes and were a perfect match for a duet event, and decided to pair them. The two swimmers had similar body types, the skills in flexibility and endurance that were necessary during a performance, and the ability to communicate with each other. While performing, both swimmers projected the impression they were mirror images of each other.

Carolyn and Michelle were an incredible duo and won nearly every major duet competition between 1985 and 1987. During the 1986 World Aquatic Championships, Carolyn Waldo won a solo gold, the Waldo and Cameron duet won gold, and the Aquabelles won gold. This was the first time a country had won all three events since 1975.

In 1988, at the Seoul Olympics, Waldo and Cameron were favoured to win gold and they did not disappoint Canada and their fans. Using their powerful manoeuvres, the Canadian duo built an incredible lead in the compulsories and swam well in their free routine to win gold.

Carolyn Waldo was also a dominating force in the solo event in synchronised swimming and brought home the gold. This made her the first Canadian female athlete to win two Olympic gold medals at a single Olympics.

Carolyn received the Bobbie Rosenfield Trophy as Canada's top female athlete in 1987 and 1988, and was awarded the Lou Marsh trophy as Canada's finest athlete in 1998. Both swimmers were inducted into Canada's Sports Hall of Fame and received the Order of Canada. After the Seoul Olympics, both swimmers retired from competitive swimming. ✪

Carolyn Waldo and Michelle Cameron

Name: _____   Date: _____

Reading Skills

Answer the following questions with complete sentences.

1. What are the three main elements a synchronized swimmer must possess in order to be successful?
   _____
   _____
   _____

2. Why is it incredible that Caroline Waldo excelled as a synchronized swimmer?
   _____
   _____

3. What spectacular Canadian historical sporting event took place in 1986?
   _____
   _____
   _____

4. Why did Debbie Muir put Carolyn Waldo and Debbie Cameron together as a duet in synchronized swimming?
   _____
   _____
   _____
   _____

5. How do you know that Debbie Muir was a good synchronized swimming coach?
   _____
   _____
   _____

6. How do you know Carolyn Waldo and Michelle Cameron were a successful synchro duet?
   _____
   _____
   _____

7. In what ways was Carolyn Waldo a dynamic solo synchro swimmer?
   _____
   _____
   _____
   _____

Vocabulary Skills

A. Using a straight line match each word to its meaning.

1. dominate   • a quality belonging to a person
2. precise   • demonstration of required skills
3. synchronize   • not stiff; easily bent
4. uncanny   • to control or rule
5. attribute   • able to withstand hard wear
6. flexibility   • exact, accurate, definite
7. endurance   • skills in a sport
8. manoeuvre   • strange and mysterious
9. technical   • happen at the same time
10. compulsories   • a skillful movement

B. Skim through the biography to find a synonym for each of the following words.

1. taught _____
2. same _____
3. talk _____
4. reflection _____
5. outstanding _____
6. moves _____
7. learn _____
8. intelligence _____
9. almost _____
10. amazing _____

C. Skim through the biography to find an antonym for each of the following words.

1. different _____
2. below _____
3. lost _____
4. destroyed _____
5. weak _____
6. minor _____

*B*obbie Rosenfeld was one of the 20th Century's greatest female athletes. She was an all-round athlete who played on basketball, hockey, softball, and lacrosse teams as well as performed as a track athlete. All of her accomplishments were done at a time when it was deemed unlady-like and even unhealthy for young women.

Fanny Rosenfeld was born in Russia on December 29, 1903 and died in Toronto on November 14, 1969. She came to Canada as an infant and was raised in Barrie, Ontario. During high school, she led her high school basketball team at Barrie Collegiate to a league championship, excelled in track, and her favourite sport was ice hockey. One day, Fanny decided to have her long hair cut off or "bobbed" so it would not be a nuisance while she participated in sports, hence her nickname "Bobbie." Even though many negative comments were made about women involved in sports, Bobbie persisted with the support and encouragement of her family. Her father was often seen cheering wildly at various sporting events.

In 1922, Bobbie's family moved to Toronto where Bobbie quickly made her presence felt in the city's athletic community. While working as a secretary at a chocolate factory, Bobbie joined the company's athletic club as well as the hockey and basketball teams. In 1923, while attending a sporting event in Beaverton, Ontario, one of her teammates convinced her to compete in the 100 yard dash. Bobbie agreed and won the race, beating the Canadian sprinting champion.

Throughout the 1920s, Bobbie dominated athletic events. In 1923, she defeated the 100 yard world champion sprinter Helen Finkley, won the 1924 Toronto grass-courts tennis championship, helped several teams get into championship competitions, and tied her running rival Rosa Grosse for the world 100 yard dash record, with a time of 11 seconds flat. In 1925, at the Ontario Ladies Track and Field Championships, Bobbie won the shot put, the discus, the running broad jump, the 200 yard dash, and the 100 yard low hurdles. She also placed second in the 100 yard dash and the javelin.

In 1928, track and field events were open to women for the first time at the Olympics. Bobbie was an integral part of the "Matchless Six," Canada's first and most famous national women's track team. In the 100 meter race, Bobbie won a silver medal and the track team claimed the gold medal in a record time of 48.2 seconds.

Bobbie was also entered in the 800 meter event although she had never trained as a distance runner. She was there to help and support Jean Thomson, a fellow teammate of the track team, who was injured and ailing. During the race, when Thomson began to weaken, Bobbie ran beside her and encouraged her to keep going. Thomson made a remarkable fourth place finish while Bobbie claimed fifth. Many observers felt Bobbie could have easily made the podium herself.

Unfortunately, Bobbie's athletic career ended a year after the Olympics when she was stricken with severe arthritis. Bobbie's athletic spirit lived on in her coaching and as a sports writer. Her column, which ran for 20 years, often promoted, encouraged, and defended women's sports.

Bobbie Rosenfeld considered her greatest victory came the day she was voted Canada's female athlete of the half century by the Canadian Press in 1950. This honour proved that she had truly left her mark on the athletic world and helped to change the existing attitude towards women in sports. Today, the Bobbie Rosenfeld award is given annually to Canada's top female athlete. ✪

Bobbie Rosenfeld

Name: _____ Date: _____

Reading Skills

Answer each question with a good sentence.

1. Why do you think people considered it unlady-like for women to participate in sports in the early 1900s? _____
_____
_____

2. How has this early attitude changed since then? _____
_____
_____

3. Why was 1928 an important year in Bobbie Rosenfeld's career? _____
_____
_____

4. How successful were the Canadian women in their first Olympics? _____
_____
_____

5. How did Bobbie show great sportsmanship during the Olympics? _____
_____
_____

6. Why was Bobbie thrilled with the honour bestowed on her by the Canadian Press in 1950? _____
_____
_____

7. Why will Bobbie Rosenfeld's name live on forever? _____
_____

Vocabulary Skills

A. In each word underline its base word.

1. accomplishments
2. greatest
3. unhealthy
4. championship
5. favourite
6. bobbed
7. encouragement
8. dominated
9. remarkable
10. annually

B. Circle the word that doesn't belong in each group. Explain why.

1. shaved   bobbed   cut   trimmed
_____

2. bother   nuisance   helpful   problem
_____

3. cheering   whispering   shouting   yelling
_____

4. won   defeat   defend   beat
_____

5. friend   rival   enemy   opponent
_____

6. dash   sprint   run   walk
_____

C. Complete each word with the correct vowel combination.

(ai, oa, ee, ea)

1. t ____ m
2. d ___ med
3. unh ___ lthy
4. r ___ sed
5. agr ___ d
6. br ___ d
7. tr ___ ned
8. ___ ling

Beth Underhill is an accomplished athlete and one of the best known in the world of Canadian show jumping. She competes in a sport in which women are equal to men, and rides for the Canadian Show Jumping Team. With the help of her equine partners, she has been victorious during many equestrian events and competitions.

Beth was born in Guelph, Ontario on September 5, 1962. When she was seven, her parents enrolled her in riding lessons at a YMCA camp in Georgetown during the summer. At the age of 14, Beth joined the Toronto-North York Pony Club and learned the different forms of riding. She enjoyed the eventing, the games, and the dressage but was very intrigued with the sport of show jumping. At the age of 15, Beth decided to concentrate her efforts on it.

Due to their daughter's new passion, Beth's parents purchased a farm shortly after her competitive career was underway. During high school, Beth competed throughout Ontario at various show jumping events. After completing high school, Beth decided to sell her horse and move to Edmonton, Alberta to ride with Mark Larkin. While working with Larkin, she found a horse called Sagan, who was a veteran jumper. On Sagan, Beth learned to develop an eye for accuracy while having Sagan jump. If she got him to the right spot, he would jump anything but if their approach was wrong, Sagan would stop and Beth would fall off. Finally, patience and persistence won a grand prix for the rider and horse.

Beth returned to Ontario with Sagan and in 1984 and 1986, they won the Ontario Open Jumper Competitions. Eager to learn more, Beth took a job with Torchy Miller. During the 1989-1990 season Beth found Monopoly, a New Zealand thoroughbred. It took Beth months of training to get to know his personality and how they could be successful together.

In 1990, the team came together and during that summer, Beth and Monopoly won the $25,000.00 DuMaurier at Bromont, Quebec. During Monopoly's show jumping career, he won over $1 million dollars and was a star in the Canadian

show jumping world with a huge fan base. In 2001, Monopoly was retired and lives at Beth's stable.

Beth's partnership with Monopoly brought many opportunities and challenges her way. She became a sponsored rider as well as riding horses for various owners. In 1994, Beth tried out a horse in Europe called Altair. He was a Dutch warm blood who stood 16.3 hands high and Beth felt he was the most incredible horse that she had ever sat on. Altair was very expensive and Beth did not want to leave him behind, so she found investors to buy him and brought Altair to Canada.

Altair was a challenge to train and to get to know, but Beth did enjoy great success competing at the World Equestrian Games in Rome, in 1998. They were also a part of the Canadian team that won a bronze medal at the 1999 Pan American Games. In the same year, Altair and Beth finished second in the richest show jumping event in the world, the $800,000 Du Maurier International at the Spruce Meadows Masters Tournament, where Beth was also named the "Leading Lady Rider." During a show in Monterray, California, Altair suffered an injury and in 2006, following a sudden illness, had to be put down.

Beth now competes with Magdaline, a mare. Together, they have won several important events. Beth feels the life of a professional rider has its ups and downs but the thrill of competition and the partnership between horse and rider are very rewarding. ✪

Beth Underhill

Name: _____   Date: _____

Reading Skills

1. In what ways is Beth Underhill's chosen sport different from most athletes? _____
   _____
   _____
   _____

2. What does an equestrian rider have to do with its equine partner before they can compete? _____
   _____
   _____

3. What qualities must a rider have in order to train a horse? _____
   _____
   _____
   _____

4. How successful was Beth Underhill with her horse Monopoly? _____
   _____
   _____
   _____

5. What further opportunities did Beth have after her partnership with Monopoly? _____
   _____
   _____
   _____

6. On which horse did Beth finish second in the richest show jumping event in the world? _____
   _____
   _____

7. How did Beth acquire Altair? _____
   _____
   _____
   _____

8. What would be some of the dangers a rider must be prepared to face during an event?
   _____
   _____
   _____

Vocabulary Skills

A. **Record each word in the box on the line beside its meaning.**

equine	equestrian	victorious
dressage	persistence	accuracy
eventing	thoroughbred	approach
investors	personality	intrigued

1. holding fast to a purpose _____

2. like a horse _____

3. qualities that make a person different
   _____

4. on horseback, mounted on a horse
   _____

5. pure breed or stock _____

6. equestrian competition _____

7. to excite one's curiosity _____

8. having no errors _____

9. having a victory, conquering _____

10. to come near or close _____

11. guidance of a horse through steps without the use of reins or noticeable signals
    _____

12. a person who invests money _____

B. **Skim through the biography to locate antonyms for the following words.**

1. cheap _____
2. stallion _____
3. poorest _____
4. cold _____
5. small _____
6. right _____
7. same _____
8. man _____

Answer Key

Scott, Burka, Magnussen, Manley: Page 6
Reading Skills:
1. Liz Manley 2. Karen Magnussen 3. Barbara Ann Scott 4. Petra Burka 5. Barbara Ann Scott 6. Liz Manley 7. Karen Magnussen 8. Barbara Ann Scott 9. Liz Manley 10. Petra Burka
Vocabulary Skills:
A. 1. sensational 2. dazzling 3. imperfections 4. dynamo 5. vivacious 6. spectacular 7. contender 8. celebrity
B. 1. Her (wonderful) performances, (girlish) beauty and (sparkling) personality captured the hearts and fans around the world.
2. Karen Magnussen was a (bright) and (vivacious) girl from Vancouver.
C. 1. contend 2. nation 3. sense 4. wonder 5. girl 6. dazzle 7. perfect

Cindy Klassen: Page 8
Reading Skills:
1. Her goal was to play on
2. Things were moving along as she
3. Her parents encouraged her to take
4. When Cindy was younger, she and
5. Much to her surprise, Cindy found
6. In a year, Cindy was on
7. While rounding a corner, Cindy crashed
8. Everyone felt that Cindy's skating season
9. Cindy Klassen will go down in
Vocabulary Skills:
A. 1. negative, positive 2. easy, difficult 3. happy, depressed 4. strong, weak 5. most, least
B. Possible Answers: energetic, avid athlete, courageous, fearless, able to focus, positive, goal oriented, determined, successful, hardworking, thinker, fighter
Research Skills: Answers will vary.

Sandra Schmirler: Page 10
Reading Skills:
1. False 2. True 3. False 4. False 5. True 6. True 7. True 8. False 9. True 10. False
Vocabulary Skills:
A. Order of words in the paragraph.
team, two, players, rectangular, turns, granite, target, house, sweepers, brooms, second, skip
B. 1. (A) 2. (S) 3. (H) 4. (A) 5. (S) 6. (H) 7. (H) 8. (S) 9. (A) 10. (S)

Myriam Bedard: Page 12
Reading Skills:
1. A biathlon competition is a cross-country race on skis while shooting at targets.
2. An athlete must be physically and mentally strong.
3. A biathlete must study the course and plan every part of the race before it takes place.
4. The weather and how the biathlete feels physically and mentally.
5. She had to improve her skiing skills and strengthen her upper body.
6. She needed money to buy a custom rifle and to pay for coaching.
7. Her agent worked out a deal with her employer for funding.
8. She won two gold medals.

Vocabulary Skills:
A. 1. issue 2. stature 3. prone 4. superior 5. premier 6. sprints 7. unpredictable 8. negotiate
B. 1. increase 2. superior 3. senior 4. freedom 5. shortest 6. lower
C. 1. compete 2. contest 3. athlete 4. equip 5. physical 6. predict

Karen Cockburn: Page 14
Reading Skills:
1. She is able to land flips exactly where she wants them on the trampoline.
2. Karen has a strong competitive drive that gives her the energy to perform difficult routines.
3. She used a trampoline during her training in diving.
4. Answers will vary.
5. She is part of a women's synchronized trampoline team.
6. They have won eight world cups in a row and captured gold at the 2007 World Championships.
7. She has won nine national titles, an Olympic bronze, two Olympic silver medals and dozens of World Cup medals.
8. She carried the Canadian flag during the closing ceremonies.
Vocabulary Skills:
A. 1. (3) 2. (5) 3. (3) 4. (4) 5. (4) 6. (4) 7. (4) 8. (3) 9. (4) 10. (3)
B. 1. legend 2. trampoline 3. surgery 4. simulate 5. synchonized 6. biography 7. reconstructive 8. seriously
Research Skills:
1. George Nissen
2. He watched trapeze artists bouncing into somersaults and other moves in the safety netting.
3. Must take off and land with either their feet, seat, front, or back. Moves must be performed in 3 basic shapes: tucked, piked or straight.

Elaine Tanner: Page 16
Reading Skills:
1. She earned many medals at various competitions and broke many swimming records.
2. Answers will vary.
3. She had a fast start, a competitive drive, and was a natural in the water.
4. They stood on the podium while Canada's new flag was raised for the first time at an International Games.
5. They shouted, cheered, and stamped their feet.
6. She listened to her coach and swam the way he instructed.
7. Answers will vary.
8. She never forgave herself for losing the gold medal. She lost her self-esteem.
9. Answers will vary.
Vocabulary Skills:
A. 1. backstroke 2. teammates 3. freestyle 4. butterfly 5. Commonwealth
B. 1. flag 2. medal 3. team 4. pool 5. podium
C. 1. Canada 2. Jamaica 3. Winnipeg or Vancouver 4. Mexico City 5. Olympics
D. 1. biggest 2. stature 3. natural 4. talent 5. traumatized 6. allowed 7. enormous 8. nervous

Chantal Petitclerc: Page 18

Reading Skills:

1. paralyzed, barn, door
2. swimming, strength, stamina
3. homemade, wheelchair
4. sprints, marathons
5. Barcelona, two, bronze
6. Paralympic, United States, gold, silver
7. Sydney, two, silver
8. Athens, Beijing, gold
9. athlete, social, history
10. role, model

Vocabulary Skills:

A. 1. remarkable 2. hardest 3. trailing 4. international
5. swimming 6. recovery 7. specialist 8. successful

B. 1. par - a - lyzed 2. in - ter- view 3. com - pet - i - tor
4. de - ter - min - a - tion 5. in - di - vid - u - al 6. mar - a - thons

C. 1. waist, wheelchair, where, won, world
2. farm, first, former, friends, future
3. specialist, sports, stamina, status, strength
4. many, marathons, medals, meter, middle
5. career, coach, collection, competed, competitors

Silken Laumann: Page 20

Reading Skills:

1. Her sister encouraged her to try it.
2. Her rowing skills quickly advanced her to a competitive level.
3. She became recognized after she earned a gold medal at the World Championships in 1991.
4. Silken was named Canada's Outstanding Athlete of 1991.
5. Her leg was badly damaged in a sculling accident.
6. She continued to train in her hospital bed. She insisted she be put in her racing scull and trained with a big brace on her leg. Silken competed at the Barcelona, Olympics.
7. She competed in the 1996 Olympic Games in Atlanta, Georgia for the last time and won the silver medal.
8. Answers will vary.

Vocabulary Skills:

A.

B	A	E	Z	S	C	A	L	D	O	N	T	K	L
D	F	D	A	C	I	E	W	V	X	U	S	M	R
F	H	B	G	A	C	T	N	A	C	S	F	H	P
A	S	C	A	B	J	E	K	G	B	Y	D	G	J
P	C	B	O	B	D	L	N	H	E	I	Z	Q	A
Q	A	W	C	A	V	R	L	M	I	S	J	W	Y
T	F	R	M	R	U	A	K	L	V	C	A	Z	X
P	F	O	S	D	U	C	B	A	C	O	B	D	E
R	O	T	N	F	G	S	C	A	L	L	O	P	K
B	L	Q	C	F	G	H	C	I	M	D	J	L	A
S	D	F	E	D	I	S	H	D	B	F	I	K	L
J	Q	R	R	S	S	C	A	L	P	G	J	N	M
N	K	A	T	U	W	A	X	C	E	H	H	O	P
L	S	C	A	P	E	L	Y	D	S	C	A	R	E
M	O	S	P	V	Z	E	A	B	E	F	G	C	A

B. 1. scalp 2. scabbard 3. scallop 4. scapel 5. scant 6. scare
7. scarf 8. scarlet 9. scale 10. scold 11. scab 12. scaffold
13. scald

Perdita Felicien: Page 22

Reading Skills:

1. She began at Pineridge Secondary School in Pickering.
2. She won the Ontario High School Hurdling Championships in 1997 and 1998.
3. She won the Canadian Junior Championships in hurdling.
4. She had several athletic scholarships offered to her by various universities.
5. She chose the University of Illinois and she studied Kinesiology.
6. Kinesiology is the science of how the body functions and moves. Answers will vary.
7. She won gold at the hurdling event at the World Championships.
8. She failed to clear a hurdle and crashed into an athlete in the adjacent lane.
9. Answers will vary.

Vocabulary Skills:

									F		
				B	U	R	S	T			
						R		U			
								R			
						B		T			
						U		L			
				P	U	R	P	L	E		
	M					G					
	U		T			L					
	R		U			A					
H	A	M	B	U	R	G	E	R			
	U		K								
S	P	U	R	S							
	U		E								
N	U	R	S	E							
	S										
	E										

Research Skills:

Answers will vary. Possible Answers: rhythmic pattern, speed, elongated sprint stride, good technique, mobility, poise, stamina, long legs, strength

Nancy Green: Page 24

Reading Skills:

1. three 2. 1958 3. Grenoble Olympics 4. Anne Heggtveit
5. Squaw Valley Olympics 6. Innsbruck Olympics
7. international competitions 8. twelve titles 9. February 15, 1968 10. skied aggressively 11. a month before the Olympics
12. scoreboard didn't come on

Vocabulary Skills:

A. 1. slopes 2. trophy 3. elite 4. thrilled 5. final 6. blistering
7. alluding 8. defeating 9. results 10. pace 11. repair 12. chance

B . 1. verb 2. phrase 3. noun 4. adjective 5. noun 6. adverb
7. verb 8. verb 9. adjective 10. preposition

Research Skills: Answers will vary.

Answer Key

Beckie Scott: Page 26
Reading Skills:

1. at the age of 13 or when a new coach came to town
2. Torino Olympics in 2006
3. at the age of 5
4. Salt Lake City Olympic Games in 2002
5. at the Junior National Championships
6. Olympic Games in Nagano, 1998
7. two and a half years later
8. Salt Lake City Olympics in 2002
9. in June of 2003
10. at the age of 7

Vocabulary Skills:

A. 1. brilliant 2. active 3. potential 4. succeed 5. fair 6. positive
7. donate 8. maid

B. Answers will vary.

Research Skills: Answers will vary.

Abigail (Abby) Hoffman: Page 28
Reading Skills:

1. There were no teams for girls in the Toronto area.
2. She made herself look like a boy by cutting her hair short and used the name Ab Hoffman when she registered.
3. She got selected for an all-star team and had to show her birth certificate.
4. Answers will vary.
5. Answers will vary.
6. She chose to compete as a middle-distance runner in track and field.
7. She competed in four Olympics, won eight national titles, set Canadian records and won medals in many other competitions.
8. She worked hard to gain recognition for elite female athletes at the university, national, and international level.

Vocabulary Skills:

A. 1. compete 2. fortunate 3. qualify 4. limit 5. special 6. accept
7. ceremony 8. nation

B. Answers will vary.

C. Answers will vary.

Hayley Wickenheiser: Page 30
Reading Skills:
Sequential Order: 4, 8, 3, 1, 11, 7, 2, 6, 10, 5, 9
Vocabulary Skills:

A. 1. (A) 2. (S) 3. (A) 4. (S) 5. (H) 6. (H) 7. (A) 8. (A) 9. (S) 10. (S)
B. 1. role 2. beat 3. thyme 4. team 5. bean 6. teem 7. beet 8. been
9. roll 10. time

Marnie McBean and Kathleen Heddle: Page 32
Reading Skills:

1. McBean 2. McBean and Heddle 3.Heddle 4. McBean and Heddle 5. McBean 6. McBean and Heddle 8. McBean 9. McBean 10. McBean and Heddle 11. McBean 12. Heddle

Vocabulary Skills:

A. 1. quarry 2. quiz 3. quantity 4. quench 5. quarrel 6. quaint
7. quality 8. quail 9. queer 10. quest 11. quirk 12. quake

B. Answers must display the meanings.

Catriona Le May Doan: Page 34
Reading Skills:
1. False 2. True 3. False 4. False 5. True 6. True
7. False 8. False 9. True 10. True 11. False 12. True
Vocabulary Skills: A.

```
R Z E S H Y S K E P T I C A L
A S K I N F U M M V L K H W U
C K A D Q N P G Q T I R C J X
O A B B T P V S N S K I T J S
K T J L C O K P L A O E L K
L E T M L R Q E N O K M K Z Y
I B H M U P D I U W O B S H X
T O S G K S F N E V A P N Q J
N A O R S Q N C L F B O I G H
P R U R D K M I Z Y T G C X S
Q D R V S Z N J L E W H J R K
G T U S W E L Y L M E K D G U
V H U W X U V E X T Y I Z S N
W V K T X C K Z H S K A T F K
F X W J Y S F B C A N C E A F
I E Y D Z Q A B O P C D E D B
```

B. 1. skat 2. skateboard 3. skein 4. skeleton 5. skeptical 6. sketch
7. skin 8. skit 9. skull 10. skunk

Beverly Boys and Sylvie Bernier: Page 36
Reading Skills:
1. Bev Boys 2. Sylvie Bernier 3. Bev Boys 4. Bev Boys
5. Sylvie Bernier 6. Bev Boys 7. Sylvie Bernier 8. Bev Boys
9. Sylvie Bernier 10. Bev Boys 11. Sylvie Bernier 12. Bev Boys
Vocabulary Skills:

Beverly **B**oys and **S**ylvie **B**ernier were famous **C**anadian female divers. They both competed in the **O**lympic **G**ames, the **C**ommonwealth **G**ames, and were **C**anadian champions. **B**everly **B**oys dove from the 10 meter tower and the 3 meter springboard while **S**ylvie **B**ernier only competed on the 3 meter springboard. Both divers each won many different coloured medals, but **S**ylvie **B**ernier was the only one to bring home an **O**lympic gold medal in diving. Both divers were honoured with the **B**obbie **R**osenfeld **A**ward.

Research Skills: Answers will vary.

Vickie Keith: Page 38
Reading Skills:

1. A person who swims long distances in large outdoor bodies of water.
2. Answers will vary. Possible Answers: strong body, strong mind, stamina, strength, speed, mental resolve, training, able to stand cold temperatures.
3. Answers will vary. Possible answers. dangers in open waters, rip tides, under tows, waves, bad weather, cold waters, rough waters, exhaustion, muscle injury, eels, cramping
4. oceans, bays, lakes, rivers, straits, channels, seas
5. Answers will vary. Possible Answers: swam in many bodies of water, holds 16 world records, swam to raise money for disabled children
6. Answers will vary.

Answer Key

Vocabulary Skills:

A. 1. ability 2. swim 3. continue 4. assist 5. able 6. arrive
   7. province 8. aware

B. worldwide, sunshine, lifetime, butterfly

C. 1. dis-a-bil-i-ties 2. for-tu-nate-ly 3. swim-ming 4. par-tic-i-pat-ed
   5. am-pu-tee 6. de-par-ture 7. in-te-grat-ed 8. dis-a-bled

D. Answers will vary but must display the meaning of the word.

Carolyn Waldo and Michelle Cameron: Page 40

Reading Skills:

1. A synchronized swimmer must have athletic ability, precise performance and communication skills.
2. She almost drowned when she was three and had to overcome her fear of the water.
3. Canada won gold medals in solo, duet, and team synchronized swimming.
4. The two swimmers had similar body types, skills in flexibility and endurance and the ability to communicate to each other while performing.
5. She had coached the Aquabelles who had won six out of eight national championships.
6. They won nearly every major duet competition between 1985 and 1987 and won gold at the Seoul Olympics.
7. She won the World Championships six times, a silver medal in the 1984 Olympic Games, and a gold medal at the 1988 Olympics.

Vocabulary Skills:

A. 1. to control or rule
   2. exact; accurate; definite
   3. happen at the same time
   4. strange and mysterious
   5. a quality belonging to a person
   6. not stiff; easily bent
   7. able to withstand hard wear
   8. a skillful movement
   9. skills in a sport
   10. demonstraton of required skills

B. 1. coached 2. similar 3. communicate 4. image 5. incredible
   6. manoeuvres 7. master 8. ability 9. nearly 10. incredible

C. 1. same 2. above 3. won 4. built 5. powerful 6. major

Bobbie Rosenfeld: Page 42

Reading Skills:

1. Answers will vary.
2. Answers will vary.
3. Women were allowed to participate in track and field events.
4. The track team won the gold medal and Bobbie won a silver medal In the 100 meter race.
5. She coached and encouraged an injured teammate to complete the 800 meter race when she could have finished in the medals.
6. Bobbie felt that she had finally helped to change the negative attitude towards women in sports.
7. Each year an outstanding Canadian female athlete is presented with the Bobbie Rosenfeld Award.

Vocabulary Skills:

A. 1. accomplish 2. great 3. health 4. champion 5. favour 6. bob
   7. courage 8. dominate 9. mark 10. annual

B. 1. shaved 2. helpful 3. whispering 4. defend 5. friend 6. walk

C. 1. team 2. deemed 3. unheathy 4. raised 5. agreed 6. broad,
   breed, braid, bread 7. trained 8. ailing

Beth Underhill: Page 44

Reading Skills:

1. In show jumping, women are equal to men and the athlete competes with a horse as a partner.
2. The rider spends hours getting to know the personality of the horse and how it likes to work.
3. Answers may vary. Possible answers: A rider must have patience, persistence, control, good work ethics, knowledge, training and leadership.
4. They won over one million dollars at different events and Monopoly was popular in the show jumping world.
5. She became a sponsored rider for various owners.
6. The horse was called Altair.
7. She had investors buy Altair and brought him to Canada so she could ride him.
8. Answers will vary.

Vocabulary Skills:

A. 1. persistence 2. equine 3. personality 4. equestrian
   5. thoroughbred 6. eventing 7. intrigued 8. accuracy 9. victorious
   10. approach 11. dressage 12. investor

B. 1. expensive 2. mare 3. richest 4. warm 5. huge 6. wrong
   7. different 8. lady